Also by Julia Floyd Jones, Ph.D.

12 Steps To Overcoming Tragic Life Events

SEEK YE FIRST THE KINGDOM OF GOD

AND HIS RIGHTEOUSNESS AND ALL THESE THINGS SHALL BE ADDED UNTO YOU
(Matthew 6:33)

BIBLICAL WORKBOOK

Dr. Julia Floyd Jones

WESTBOW
PRESS®
A DIVISION OF THOMAS NELSON
& ZONDERVAN

WestBow Press books may be ordered through booksellers or by contacting:

WestBow Press
A Division of Thomas Nelson & Zondervan
1663 Liberty Drive
Bloomington, IN 47403
www.westbowpress.com
1 (866) 928-1240

Maps from http://www.ccel.org/bible/phillips/JBPhillips.htp

ISBN: 978-1-4908-1865-8 (sc)
ISBN: 978-1-4908-1866-5 (e)

Library of Congress Control Number: 2013922022

Print information available on the last page.

WestBow Press rev. date: 6/13/2019

This book is dedicated to my sister Mary, who was always there for me to offer her support as I went through my many trials and tribulations.

For everyone who has had a "Job experience" we know that all things work together for good to them that love God, to them who are called according to his purpose. If God be for us who can be against us? We are more than conquerors! May God to continue to bless and keep each and every one of you.

Romans 8:28, 31, 37

CONTENTS

THE KINGDOM OF GOD

If you have read and worked *12 Steps To Overcoming Tragic Life Events* before starting this workbook then you have a good foundation and have developed a closer relationship with your Lord and Savior Jesus Christ. It is a manual to help you get over your past and to teach the fundamentals of Christianity. It is a book that you will refer to and teach from for many years to come. Although this current workbook is based on the same steps, with some elaboration, as in *12 Steps To Overcoming Tragic Life Events*, the approach is different and based on twelve specific books of the Bible.

In Step 12 of the manual you should have denounced your ungodly associations which connected you with the world's system. Step 12 was written to wake up your spirit man and to increase your understanding of the Kingdom of God.

Once you become born again and accept Jesus as your Lord and Savior then you become a citizen of the Kingdom with all the privileges and promises. As a citizen of the Kingdom of God, there should be reverence and honor for your ruler, God the Father, God the Son, and God the Holy Spirit (Munroe, 2006).

Now that you have denounced your ungodly associations connected with the world's system it is time for you to understand the kingdom in which you live. The kingdom of God is not a place, it is a way of living under the government of God. His rules and guidelines are found in the Bible. The Holy Spirit is your teacher and counselor and He is found inside of you as a born again believer in the Lord Jesus Christ. What can you expect from the Kingdom of God? You can expect Kingdom Promises.

The following scriptures in the book of Galatians tells us what God thinks about us and our position as His people in the Kingdom of God.

For ye are all children of God by faith in Christ Jesus. For as many of you have been baptized into Christ have put on Christ. And if ye be Christ's then are ye Abraham's seed and heirs according to the promise. And because ye are sons, God hath sent forth the Spirit of his Son into your hearts, crying, Abba, Father. Wherefore thou art no more a servant but a son, and if a son, then an heir of God through Christ (Galatians 3:26,27, 29; 4:6,7).

Accessing Your Inheritance In The Kingdom Of God
Come Up Higher

As a citizen of the Kingdom we are heirs to the throne and have access to the throne room because of Jesus Christ who sits on the right hand of God. This is explained in the following scriptures. *And hath raised us up together, and made us sit together in heavenly places in Chirst Jesus. For through him we both have access by one spirit unto the Father. Now therefore ye are no more strangers and foreigners, but fellow citizens with the saints and of the household of God (Ephesians 2:6, 18, 19).* We are saints in the household of God. Do you understand? We are privileged, we are royalty and we don't have to wait until somebody dies to receive our inheritance. That was already done at the cross, to the glory of God. Jesus died so that we can receive our inheritance right now.

As children and heirs of God we have everything that belongs to our Father. All we have to do is ask. Look at what the scripture says in Jeremiah 33:3. *Call unto me, and I will answer thee and show thee great and mighty things which thou knowest not.* How is the Father going to show us these things? The Lord has given us the ability to ascend and descend to the throne room for instruction and revelation through dreams, visions, and by being in the spirit. Some of you may be familiar with the following scriptures in the Book of Genesis which is commonly referred to as Jacob's ladder. It talks about ascending and descending.

And he dreamed and behold a ladder set up on the earth and the top of it reached to heaven and behold the angels of God ascending and descending on it. And behold the Lord stood above it and said I am the Lord God of Abraham (Genesis 28:12-13).

Angels are not the only beings that have the ability to ascend and descend. Believers are allowed to ascend into the throne room in the spirit. The Book of Revelation was revealed to the Apostle John while he was in the spirit. This is not astral projection where you will your soul to leave your body. This is about your born-again spirit moving through the kingdom of heaven as the Lord allows.

I was in the Spirit on the Lord's day and heard behind me a great voice as of a trumpet, saying,

I am the Alpha and Omega, the first and the last and what thou seest write in a book. After this I looked and behold a door was opened in heaven and the first voice which I heard was as it were of a trumpet talking with me, which said, come up hither, and I will show thee things which must be hereafter. And immediately I was in the spirit and behold a throne was set in heaven and one sat on the throne (Revelation 1:10, 11, 4:1, 2).

When will you ascend? Let the Holy Spirit take you there!

The Promises of God

God's promises are written in scripture, bound by covenant, hoped for through faith, and spoken in prophecy. The promises of God are also expressed as the blessings of God. We will study the blessings of God, referred to as the beatitudes, found in the book of Matthew, which corresponds to Step 8 in this workbook.

God promised that we believers can have everything He has. As a citizen of the kingdom we should also reflect everything that God is. When we ask Jesus to come into our heart as a born again believer, then the Holy Spirit takes up residence inside of us giving us access to everything that He is. That means that we can take on his character as evidenced by the fruit of the Spirit as explained in Galatians 5:22-23. *But the fruit of the Spirit is love, joy, peace, longsuffering (patience), gentleness, goodness, faith, meekness, and temperance (self-control).*

There are nine parts to the one fruit of the Spirit and these characteristics are what every born-again believer should strive to develop as we mature in our Christian walk with the Lord. Of course the fruit of the Spirit takes time to develop and must be practiced throughout our life if it is to manifest, take hold, and arrest the negative aspects of our soul condition. In order for the fruit of the Spirit to take root it needs to be planted in good soil. Commit the following Bible verses to memory and watch your fruit grow in the city of your soul.

Love	*And to know the love of Christ which passeth knowledge that ye might be filled with all the fullness of God (Ephesians 3:19).*
Joy	*The redeemed of the Lord shall return and come with singing unto Zion and everlasting joy shall be upon their head (Isaiah 51:11)*
Peace	*Peace I leave with you, my peace I give unto you, not as the world giveth, give I unto you. Let not your heart be troubled, neither let it be afraid (John 14:27).*

Long Suffering (Patience)	*Let us run with patience the race that is set before us (Hebrews 12:1b)*
Gentleness	*The servant of the Lord must not strive but be gentle unto all men (2 Timothy 2:24)*
Goodness	*The earth is full of the goodness of the Lord (Psalm 33:5)*
Faith	*But without faith it is impossible to please him, for he that cometh to God must believe that he is, and that he is a rewarder of them that diligently seek him (Hebrews 11:6).*
Meekness	*Blessed are the meek for they shall inherit the earth (Matthew 5:5).*
Temperance (Self-Control)	*I can do all things through Christ who strengthens me (Phillipians 4:13).*

Spiritual Gifts

Because of our covenant relationship with the Lord, Jesus Christ, we have been given promises of God through spiritual gifts. I Corinthians 12:8-10 explains the gifts of the Spirit that are available to every believer. Through the Holy Spirit, Christians have access to the supernatural gifts of: the word of wisdom, the word of knowledge, faith, healing, working of miracles, prophecy, discerning of spirits, diverse kinds of tongues, and the interpretation of tongues. These gifts are not for us but work through us to help others. It is up to the Holy Spirit to decide what gifts are to be given to the spirit of the believer. If you are not aware of your Spiritual gifts, ask the Holy Spirit to reveal them to you. Sometimes they are just lying dormant waiting to be activated.

It is my prayer that by the time you have completed this workbook your gifts will have been revealed to you through scripture, revelation knowledge, or through a dream. Perhaps the answer will come through an apostle, prophet, evangelist, pastor, or teacher (Ephesians 4:11). Be open to receive the message from the Lord in whatever way He decides to reveal it to you.

Provisions

God takes care of his children. He has provided everything we need. Sometimes people go without necessary provisions simply because they have not asked the Father for what they need. Provisions are available to us because we are our heirs to the throne of God through Jesus Christ. The following scriptures will help you to pray and receive from the Lord.

Ask and it shall be given you, seek and ye shall find, knock and it shall be opened unto you. For everyone that seeketh findeth, and to him that knocketh it shall be opened (Matthew 7:7-8).

And seek not what ye shall eat, or what ye shall drink, neither be ye of doubtful mind. For all these things do the nations of the world seek after and your Father knoweth that ye have need of these things. But rather seek ye the kingdom of God and all these things shall be added unto you (Luke 12:29-31). Ask the Father for what you need in prayer, ask Him now.

Faith

The world says "seeing is believing." The Word of God says *the just shall live by faith. Now faith is the substance of things hoped for, the evidence of things not seen (Hebrews 10:38, 11:1).* Through faith we access our promises and provisions from God. Abraham was a man who lived by faith. (Read Romans 4:12-25). God promised Abraham that he would be the father of many nations when he was almost a hundred years old. Even though by worldly standards Abraham and Sarah were too old to conceive and bear a child, the Bible says that Abraham staggered not at the promises of God through unbelief. What has God promised you? Stagger not!

The Lord has given many gifts to the body of Christ so that we may prosper, be in good health, and win against the attacks of the enemy. God's promises come in many forms such as earthly provisions, spiritual gifts, and covenant relationships. If we practice the fruit of the Spirit, pray, listen, and obey, then we will receive our blessings in God's timing. This workbook was written to help believers live in the Kingdom of God with all the provisions and covenant promises that the Lord has provided.

When God gives you a promise, hold on to it by faith. *For all the promises of God in him are yea, and in him Amen unto the glory of God by us (2 Corinthiams 1:20).*

WORKING THE STEPS

Now that you have a basic understanding of the Kingdom of God, it is time to go deeper into the word of God. Each step corresponds with a book of the Bible. This is a very extensive study of twelve books of the Bible. Multiple questions are asked for each chapter. It is important to answer all of them and to take your time. Don't be surprised if you are unable to complete the workbook in less than six months. This type of study is to ensure that you receive true intimacy with the most High God, understand the Kingdom of God, and obtain the promises of God.

As a result of this study, questions will be answered in your personal life and relationships will be healed. It will prepare the way for deliverance and healing of the soul and body. Below are the 12 steps and the corresponding books of the Bible:

Step 1 Ephesians   Step 7 Revelations

Step 2 Acts   Step 8 Matthew

Step 3 Lamentations   Step 9 Daniel

Step 4 Genesis   Step 10 James

Step 5 Psalm   Step 11 Phillippians

Step 6 Exodus   Step 12 Job

In His infinite wisdom, the Lord has given us six books from the Old Testament and six books from the New Testament. It is important to understand how the Christian faith came down through the generations, the Hebraic roots of our faith, the covenants, as well as the duplicity, and other character defects of fallen man. Do not lose hope, all is well. The Most High God was able to redeem mankind through the blood of the Lamb, Jesus Christ the last and final sacrifice.

Hold on to your seat! You are in for the ride of your life, for your life!

DIRECTIONS:

Read each book one chapter at a time. After you have finished reading the chapter, go back and answer the questions for that chapter. The answers to the questions are in the verses provided in parentheses after each question to ensure accuracy.

The King James Version of the Bible was used to write the study questions. To avoid confusion, use a bible that matches exactly chapter and verse with the King James Version. There are many study bibles available but use them sparingly. The annotated versions may lead you to a conclusion that is contrary to what the Lord is speaking to you right now, a word that is relevant to your situation, a word in due season. This will become evident if you are working these steps with a group. Many of you will get different revelations from the same verse of scripture but that is the way of the Lord in this hour. It is not about interpretation, but about revelation, God speaking to you through the scriptures.

And be not conformed to this world but be ye transformed by the renewing of your mind that ye may prove what is that good and acceptable and perfect will of God. (Romans 12:2)

THE BOOK OF EPHESIANS

Step One: Say The Name - The Name Above Every Name

This book is an epistle of Apostle Paul that was circulated to all of the churches of Asia Minor. Ephesus was the major city in Asia Minor, and thus the Ephesians were the citizens of that city. The book of Ephesians explains who Jesus is, who you are as a believer, and many other biblical principles so that you can obtain true intimacy with the Lord.

Read each chapter and answer the following questions.

Chapter 1 – Predestination and Inheritance

1. Who does Paul say that he is? (1)

2. When were we chosen? (4)

3. What were we given by grace? (7)

4. What will happen in the dispensation of time? (10)

5. What is Paul praying for in verses 17 - 19?

6. Where does Christ sit in heavenly places? (20-21)

7. What name is above every name and who is the head of the church? (21-22)

Chapter 2 – Grace and Unity of Believers

1. How can one be saved and can you be saved (eternal salvation) through good works? (8-9)

2. What is God's gift in verse eight?

3. Explain what happens to those who are without Jesus Christ, strangers to the covenant of promise, and having no hope without God in the world. (1-3)

4. Once we are saved where do we sit in the spirit realm? (6)

5. What and through him will God show us in ages to come? (7)

6. How do we access our Father God? (18)

7. Once we become citizens of the kingdom what is our foundation and who is the chief cornerstone? (20)

Chapter 3 – Paul's Prayer To The Gentiles

1. What was Paul called to do? (7-8)

2. What was revealed to the Apostle Paul? (3, 9-11)

3. How do we access the Father (verse 12) and what is Paul praying for the church in verses 16 -18?

4. How does God respond to what we think about and ask for? Where is the power? (20)

Chapter 4 – The Spirit and Ascension Gifts

1. What is the message Paul is preaching to the church as written in verses 4-6?

2. After Jesus died on the cross he descended into hell, was resurrected, and then ascended into heaven. Upon his ascension, what gifts did he leave the church and for what purpose? They are also called the five-fold ministry gifts. (11-16)

3. What happens to Gentiles, those without Christ, according to verses 17-19?

4. When you have accepted Jesus Christ as Lord what should be reflected in your behavior and attitude? (23-32)

Chapter 5 – Christian Living and Marriage

1. As followers of God, how are we to walk? (2)

2. Paul has instructed the saints (Christians) how to live. (8b,14-20) What are we to stay away from? (3, 4, 5, 6, 11)

3. How are wives to treat their husbands? (21-24, 33)

4. How are husbands to treat their wives? (21, 23, 25, 28-33)

Chapter 6 – Respect for Authority and The Whole Armor of God

1. What are children instructed to do in verses 1- 3?

2. How are fathers (parents) instructed to bring up their children? (4)

3. How are servants (employees) instructed to behave toward their masters (employer)? (5-8)

4. How are masters (employers) instructed to behave toward their servants (employees)? (9)

5. How do we fight successfully against the devil? (10-11)

6. If we are not fighting against flesh and blood, then what are we fighting? (12) This is the hierarchy of the demonic realm.

7. Verses 14 - 17 are used in spiritual warfare. This is the full armor of God. Pray these scriptures out loud now and as needed. Bookmark this passage for future reference.

SUMMARY QUESTIONS

1. Who are you in Christ and what have you been called to do?

2. Do you belong to a church where the five-fold ministry gifts are in operation?

3. Do you believe in the gifts of the spirit? Why or why not?

4. What gifts has God given to you and have they been birthed into this realm of existence?

FIVE-FOLD MINISTRY GIFTS AND THEIR DEFINITIONS

And he gave some, apostles and some prophets, and some evangelists, and some pastors and teachers, for the perfecting of the saints, for the work of the ministry, for the edifying of the body of Christ (Ephesians 4:11–12).

Apostle

An apostle is appointed by God to head the church government. They are kingdom minded and promote divine order by putting ministers and others in the right positions at the right time. It is their job to train ministers and send them out to preach the gospel of the Lord Jesus Christ. On a spiritual level, they war in the stratosphere and rule over principalities.

Prophet

Prophets are commissioned by God to speak for Him, to declare His word, to reveal truths, foretell the future, and to speak life into the body of Christ.

Evangelist

Evangelists are ministers who are sent out to preach the gospel, convert non-believers to Christianity, and to win souls for Jesus Christ. Depending on the denomination, many evangelists operate in the gifts of the spirit.

Pastor

A pastor is a shepherd that tends to his flock as a minister of a local congregation. It is the pastor's job to transform the membership and free them from spiritual bondage. This is done through sermons, teaching, nurturing, love, respect, and counseling of the membership.

Teacher

In the body of Christ a teacher instructs, guides the studies, and imparts knowledge to a designated group of people about the Word of God.

(Definitions are taken from Price, 2006; Webster, 1998)

Read Ephesians 6:10-17 again in your Bible in order to get the full impact of what the Lord is telling you about the power He has given you as a Christian. Many believers avoid this type of teaching because of the fear that comes upon them when this subject is broached. That fear does not come from God. Once you understand this teaching you will be more victorious against the attacks of the enemy. How can you win the battle if you don't know who you are fighting?

Ephesians 6:12 describes the hierarchy of Satan's kingdom. The following definitions of the hierarchy were taken from a book written by Dr. Cindy Trimm called *The Rules of Engagement*.

HIERARCHY OF SATAN'S KINGDOM
Principalities

These are the highest ranking dark spirits in Satan's army and derive their power directly from Satan. They often embody world leaders so that they can influence affairs of humanity on a national level by impacting laws and policies.

Powers

These demonic spirits are second in the chain of command directly under principalities. They are commanded to destroy marriages, families, churches, education systems, and governments.

Rulers Of The Darkness Of This World

These demonic forces prey on the thoughts, feelings, and perceptions of humanity. It is their function to blind the minds of people to the truth, facilitate sin, wickedness, and iniquity within the nations of this world. They perpetuate Satan's ideals through mass media, music, movies, fashion, sports, philosophies, and religious ideologies.

Spiritual Wickedness In High Places

These spirits operate in the second heaven and prohibit the manifestation and answers to prayers of Christians. It is also their function to attack the mind of the believer by perverting and distorting perceptions, imaginations, ideologies, paradigms, and belief systems.

Fiery Darts Of The Wicked

Metaphorically speaking, fiery darts are bad attitudes, verbal abuse, or any negative thing thrown at the believer to get us off course. The fiery darts can come through anger, jealousy, and bitterness. Faith is a necessary counter-offensive for protection.

PUT ON THE FULL ARMOR OF GOD
Ephesians 6:14-17

Loins Girt About With Truth

To be victorious Christians must have knowledge of the truth of God's word.

Breastplate Of Righteousness

This symbolizes living a godly life which encompasses ethical and moral conduct.

Feet Shod With The Preparation Of The Gospel Of Peace

The Gospel of Peace frees believers from worry and anxiety. This allows us to hear the voice of God and advance against the enemy.

The Shield Of Faith

Faith enables us to believe the promises of God as written in the word of God, and spoken by the prophets of God if we doubt not.

Helmet of Salvation

This means that believers have the assurance of salvation.

The Sword Of The Spirit

The sword of the Spirit is the word of God, the written word of God found in the Bible. (The definitions about the Full Armor Of God were taken from the King James Study Bible, 1988).

Now that you understand who and what you are fighting, it has become evident that you are no match for the kingdom of Satan without using the supernatural power of the most High God that is given to every believer through Jesus Christ. Jesus is the name above every name. It is the name above every principality, power, rulers of the darkness of this world, and spiritual wickedness in high places. Use the name of Jesus, put on your full armor, and the demons will flee from you.

$\mathcal{T}$HE BOOK OF ACTS

Step Two: Confess That Jesus Is The Son Of God With Signs And Wonders Following
This book chronicles the "Acts of the Apostles" primarily Apostles Peter and Paul, and it is considered the second volume of the book of Luke. The book of Acts begins with the ascension of Jesus, the birth of the church, and the beginning of the great commission. Much more will be revealed to you as you study.

Chapter 1 – The Ascension Of Jesus And Selection Of A New Disciple

1. How many days after Jesus' crucifixion (passion) was he seen on the earth? (3)

2. Jesus told his disciples that they would be baptized by what method? (5)

3. How did the disciples receive power? What did Jesus tell them to do? This is also called the great commission. (8)

4. Where and how was Jesus taken up into heaven? (9, 12)

5. How many people gathered in the upper room in prayer and supplication in one accord? (15)

6. Which two men were being considered to be the next apostle? (23)

7. Who was chosen? (26)

Chapter 2 – The Out Pouring of the Holy Spirit and Pentecost

1. What happened on the day of Pentecost in verses 1-4?

2. What type of men showed up for this gathering and how were they able to hear the message in their native tongue? (5-16)

3. What will come to pass in the last days saith God? (17)

4. After Peter preached the gospel of Jesus Christ in verses 22-36 what did he tell the men to do? (38)

5. How many souls were saved and baptized in the Holy Spirit? (41)

6. How did the disciples continue to evangelize? (44-47)

Chapter 3 – Healing of A Lame Man And A Call To Repentance

1. Describe the man that was at the gate of the temple? (1-2)

2. What did this man ask of Peter and John and what did they give him? (3-6)

3. How was the gift received? (7-8)

4. How did the people in the temple react? (9-11)

5. Peter explained by what power the lame man was healed. (12-13)

Chapter 4 – Peter And John Preach The Gospel And Are Threatened And Released

1. Why were the priests and other people of the temple grieved? (2)

2. Approximately how many people heard the word and believed? (4)

3. The scribes and priests asked Peter and John by what power they had performed this miracle. (7) What was Peter filled with as he responded? (8)

4. What was the content of Peter's message? (10-12).

5. What type of men were Peter and John? (13)

6. Explain what the leaders decided to do about the miracle that was performed? (16-18)

7. How did the apostles respond? (29-31)

8. What mind set was among the multitude? (32)

9. What did some of the believers do with their possessions? (33-37)

Chapter 5 – Ananias And Sapphira, Signs And Wonders

1. What did Ananias and Sapphira do with their possessions? (1-2)

2. What did the Holy Ghost reveal to Peter? (3-4)

3. What happened to Ananias after Peter spoke? (5-6)

4. When did Sapphira come into the temple? (7)

5. What did she say about the price of land? (8)

6. Describe what happened to her. (10)

7. After this, what happened among the people? (11-16)

8. Explain what the Apostles went through after they were thrown in prison and what did the angel of the Lord command them to do? (19-20)

9. The high priest, captain of the prison, and officers conferred with each other about this situation. What was decided? (21-27)

10. How did Peter respond? (29)

11. How were the Apostles treated after this manner and what did they continue to do? (40-42)

Chapter 6 – The Disciples Increase In Number

1. What were the Grecians complaining about? (1)

2. What was the resolution? (3)

3. Who did they choose? (5)

4. After they prayed what did they do to the men? (6)

5. What happened because of this? (7)

6. Describe Stephen as written in verse 8.

7. Who rose up against Stephen and what did they say? (11-14)

8. For those who sat in council, how did they see Stephen's face? (15)

Chapter 7 – Stephen Preaches Before He Is Martyred

1. Summarize what Stephen preached to the council in verses 1-50.

2. After his sermon, what did he yell? (51-53)

3. How did the men respond after they heard this? (54)

4. What did the Holy Spirit allow Stephen to see? (55-56)

5. After this, what action did they take? (57-58)

6. Did Stephen live through this? (59-60)

Chapter 8 – Samaria Is Evangelized And Phillip Is Caught Away

1. After Stephen's murder, what was happening to the church at this time? Who consented to his death? (1)

2. What did the devout men do? (2)

3. What position did Saul take? (3)

4. Where did Phillip preach and what happened after he preached the word? (5-8)

5. Describe what kind of man Simon was and what the people of Samaria thought about him? (9 - 11)

6. What happened after they heard Phillip preach? (12)

7. Did Simon accept Philip's teaching and if so explain? (13)

8. Why were Peter and John sent to Samaria? (14-15)

9. What happened after they laid their hands on them? (17)

10. Why did Simon offer the Apostles money? (18,19)

11. How did Peter respond? (21-23)

12. When did the Apostles return to Jerusalem? (25)

13. What did the angel of the Lord say to Philip? (26)

14. Describe who Philip met and what they discussed (27-31)

15. What are verses 32 and 33 about?

16. After Philip preached Jesus to the Ethiopian what did the man ask for? (36)

17. Describe what happened next? (37-38)

18. How and where did the Lord take Philip? (39-40)

Chapter 9 – Saul On The Road To Damascus

1. What did Saul threaten and demand of the synagogues? (1-2)

2. Describe what happened to Saul on the road to Damascus? (3-6)

3. How did the men react that were with him? (7)

4. How long was Saul without sight and what did his diet consist of? (8-9)

5. What was Ananias commanded to do? (10-11)

6. What was he concerned about? (13-14)

7. How did the Lord respond? (15-16)

8. What happened after Ananias laid hands on Saul? (17-18)

9. What did he do after he was strengthened? (19-20)

10. How did the people react to Saul preaching the word? (21-22)

11. How did Saul escape the Jews' plot to kill him? (24-25)

12. How did the disciples in Jerusalem react to Saul? (26)

13. What was Barnabas' role? (27)

14. How did the Grecians react? (29)

15. What miracle did Peter perform in Lydda & Saron and what did the people do? (33-35)

16. Why was Peter summoned to Joppa? (36-39)

17. What four things did Peter do before Dorcus was brought back from death? (40)

Chapter 10 - Visions

1. Who was Cornelius? (1-2)

2. What did Cornelius see in his vision? (3-6)

3. What happened to Peter as he was praying? (11-16)

4. What did the Lord command Peter to preach? (42-43)

5. What type of men heard the word and what happened? (44-48)

Chapter 11- The Church in Antioch

1. How far did Stephen travel? (19)

2. Who was sent from the church in Jerusalem? (22)

3. How long did the disciples and apostles stay in Antioch? (26)

4. When were the disciples first called Christians? (26)

Chapter 12 – Herod, James, And Peter

1. Who killed James and how? (1)

2. What happened to Peter during Passover? (3-4)

3. What did the church do on his behalf? (5)

4. How was Peter being held? (6)

5. Describe what happened after the angel of the Lord appeared. (7-10)

6. In verse eleven, what did Peter realize after he came to himself?

7. Where did Peter go? (12)

8. Who answered the door and how did she react? (13-14)

9. What happened to the men who were guarding Peter? (19)

10. Why and how did Herod die? (23)

Chapter 13 – Paul And Barnabas

1. Describe who was at the church at Antioch? (1)

2. After they fasted and prayed who did the Holy Ghost separate? (2)

3. Where did they go? (4-5)

4. Who did they find on the isle of Paphos? (6)

5. What did Sergius Paulus want and what did Elymas try to do? (7-8)

6. What did Paul do to the sorcerer? (10-11)

7. How did the deputy respond? (12)

8. What did Paul preach in Antioch? (14-34)

9. What happened on the next Sabbath day? (44)

10. How did the Jews react? (45)

11. How did the gentiles receive the word? (48-49)

Chapter 14 – Signs And Wonders In Iconium And Lystra

1. What miracles happened at Lystra? (8-10)

2. How did the people respond and what names did they call Paul and Barnabas? (11-12)

3. What did the Jews from Antioch & Iconium persuade the people to do? (19)

4. How do we enter into the kingdom of God? (22)

5. Who and how did the Apostles ordain into the church? (23)

Chapter 15 – The Council At Jerusalem, Paul and Barnabas Split Up

1. What did the men from Judaea teach? (1)

2. What did Paul and Barnabas decide to do? (2)

3. What did the Pharisees believe? (5)

4. After much disputing what did Peter say? (7,8)

5. According to Peter's teaching how are our hearts purified (9) and how are we saved (11)?

6. After Barnabas and Paul spoke what did Simeon declare? (14-20)

7. How did the apostles decide to communicate the decision regarding circumcision? (23, 25, 27)

8. How did Judas and Silas use their prophetic gifts? (32)

9. What did Paul and Barnabas do in Antioch? (35)

10. What was Paul's suggestion after they finished preaching in Antioch? (36)

11. Why did Paul and Barnabas go their separate ways? (37-39)

12. Where did Barnabas go and who was his companion? (39)

13. Who did Paul travel with and where did they go? (40-41)

Chapter 16 – Lydia, Paul and Silas at midnight
1. Who was Timotheus (1) and what did Paul do to him? (3)

2. Describe Paul's vision (9).

3. What did they do on the Sabbath? (13)

4. Who was Lydia, where was she from, and what did she sell? (14) Who was baptized? (15)

5. What happened when the apostle went into prayer? (16-17)

6. Paul became grieved after many days and what did he do? (18)

7. How did her masters react to Paul and Silas after this? (19-23)

8. What did Paul and Silas do at midnight (25) and what happened next? (26)

9. Describe what happened to the prison guard. (27-34)

10. Why didn't Paul depart after the magistrate said he could leave? (37)

Chapter 17 – Those Who Turned The World Upside Down

1. What did Paul do for three Sabbath days in Thessalonica? (1-3)

2. Who believed and who did not believe what Paul preached? (4-5)

3. What was contrary to the decree of Caesar? (7)

4. Why was Paul's spirit stirred when he went to Athens? (16)

5. What type of philosophers questioned Paul's teaching? (18)

6. How did Paul respond to the altar inscription, "To The Unknown God"? (22-32)

Chapter 18 – Corinth and Ephesus

1. Why did Aquila and Priscilla depart from Rome? (2)

2. When did Paul decide to testify to the Jews in Corinth that Jesus was the Christ? (5)

3. Why did Paul leave the Jews to go among the gentiles? (6)

4. What did the Lord speak to Paul in a night vision? (9, 10)

5. How long did he stay in Corinth? (11)

6. What did the Greeks do to Sosthenes? (17)

7. Aquila, Priscilla, and Paul left Corinth went to Ephesus. In Ephesus why did Aquila and Priscilla take Apollos under their wing? (26)

8. Where did Paul go next to strengthen the disciples? (23)

Chapter 19 - Ephesus

1. When Paul went back to Ephesus what did he ask of the disciples? (2)

2. What happened after Paul laid hands on the 12 men? (6)

3. What did Paul preach for three months in the synagogues? (8)

4. What type of miracles did God perform through Paul? (12)

5. What happened when the sevens sons of Sceva and a few other men tried to exorcise demons without using the name of Jesus? (16)

6. How did this effect the Jews and Greeks in Ephesus? (17-20)

7. Why was Demetrius threatened by the preached word of God? (24-28)

8. What did the people of Ephesus cry out? (34)

Chapter 20 – Eutychus Falls And Is Healed

1. How long did Paul stay in Greece? (2,3)

2. What happened to a young man named Eutychus when Paul was preaching? (9)

3. What did Paul do and say after this? (10)

4. Summarize what Paul preached to the elders in Ephesus. (18-22)

5. What did the Holy Ghost reveal to Paul about his trip to Jerusalem? (23)

6. How was Paul going to finish what he was called to do? (24)

7. What did Paul predict would happen to this group of disciples after his permanent departure? (29-31)

8. What were the words of Christ that Paul quoted to the elders? (35)

9. Why did the elders weep? (38)

Chapter 21 – Prophecy

1. Who had four daughters and what were their gifts? (8-9)

2. What did Agabus prophecy to Paul? (11)

3. How did Paul respond to this? (13)

4. Summarize what the Jews did after they saw Paul in the temple? (27-36)

Chapter 22 – Paul Testifies

1. After Paul was chained and captured he asked to speak to the people in Hebrew. Summarize what he said. (1-21).

2. Why did the chief captain free Paul? (25-26)

Chapter 23 – Paul Before The Council

1. What did Paul perceive about the council? (6)

2. Explain what the Pharisees and Sadducees believed and the conclusion the Pharisees came to regarding this matter. (8-9)

3. What did the Lord tell Paul the following night? (11)

4. Explain the oath that the Jews took concerning Paul. (12-13)

5. Where did the centurions deliver Paul? (24, 31, 33)

6. What did the governor decide to do? (35)

Chapter 24 – Ananias, Drusila, and Felix

1. Paul was held for five days. What did the high priest, Ananias accuse him of? (5,6)

2. How did Paul defend himself? (11-15)

3. What did Paul say to Drusila and Felix? (24)

Chapter 25 - Caesarea

1. After two years Paul was still imprisoned in Caesarea. What did he say on his behalf? (8, 10)

2. What was the delay in sentencing? (16)

3. What did Festus say on Paul's behalf? (24-27)

Chapter 26 – King Agrippa

1. Why do you think Paul gave his testimony to King Agrippa in verses 4-18?

2. How did Festus respond to Paul's testimony? (24)

3. Why didn't King Agrippa set Paul free? (32)

Chapter 27 – Paul's Voyage

1. Summarize what happened on the voyage to Italy? (2-8)

2. What did Paul prophesy about the voyage? (10)

3. How did the Euroclydon winds affect the voyage? (14-16)

4. After this, what did Paul prophesy? (22)

5. What did the angel of the Lord tell him? (23-24)

6. How long did Paul and the soldiers fast? (33)

7. Why did the soldiers want to kill the prisoners? (42)

Chapter 28 – Melita and Rome

1. On what island did the ship run aground? (1)

2. What did the natives think after Paul was bitten by a viper? (4)

3. When Paul failed to die because of the snake bite, what did the natives conclude then? (6)

4. What gifts did Paul begin to operate in on this island? (8-9) Although it is not written in the scripture what can we assume happened to the people on this island after they saw the signs and wonders?

5. Summarize what Paul talked about once he got to Rome? (16-20)

6. The Jews gave him permission to speak for one day. What did Paul preach about? (23)

7. What did Paul do for the next two years in this place? (28-31)

COMPARATIVE SUMMARY OF THE APOSTLES
The Twelve Apostles Before the Day of Pentecost

Peter	James
Andrew	John
Phillip	Thomas
Bartholmew	James (son of Alphaeus)
Matthew	Judas (brother of James)
Simon	Mathias (chosen to replace Judas Iscariot)

As the Word of God was preached, many people were saved and became disciples, ministers, and prophets of God. A few of them are listed below along with some of the twelve Apostles mentioned above. As you recall, not all of the apostles were written about in the book of Acts.

The Apostles And Their Giftings In The Book of Acts

Peter
- Spoke on the day of Pentecost and explained about speaking in tongues
- Along with **John** healed a lame man by speaking the name of Jesus
- Used gift of knowledge with Ananias and Sapphira
- Signs and wonders followed as he preached, people healed by his shadow
- Healed paralyzed man in Lydda
- Rose Tabitha from the dead
- Fell into a trance on the house top in Joppa
- Preached at the home of Cornelieus and all who heard it spoke in tongues and were water baptized
- While he was in jail the church interceded for him and then he was released by an angel

Stephen (also called a deacon and an evangelist)
- Preached with signs and wonders and miracles following
- Used gift of wisdom
- The people in council saw his face as an angel
- He had an open vision of heaven before he was stoned to death

Phillip
- Went to Samaria and preached with signs and miracles following. He cast out unclean spirits, healed the lame, and baptized the converted.
- He told the Ethiopian eunuch about Christ and baptized him.
- He was translated (supernaturally transported) from Gaza to Azotus.
- He had four virgin daughters who could prophesy

Barnabus
- Took Saul (Paul) to the apostles, preached as far as Antioch.
- Disciples were first called Christians at Antioch

Barnabus and Paul

- Preached in Antioch and many Jews were saved
- They went to Iconium and preached to the Jews and Greeks, many were converted with signs and wonders following
- They went to Derbe, Lystra, Iconium, and Antioch and ordained elders in every church.

Judas and Silas

- Exhorted the brethren in Antioch with their prophetic gift

Paul and Silas

- Worshiped God with praise and song in prison and at midnight there was an earthquake, the prison doors were opened, the chains were loosed, and the guard and his family were saved.

Agabus

- A prophet from Judaea gave Paul a warning about his impending fate

Paul (Saul)

- Blinded and converted on the road to Damascus
- Preached his first message in a synagogue in Damascus
- Preached on the Sabbath in Antioch and many Jews were saved
- Blinded a sorcerer name Barjesus
- Healed a crippled man in Lystra
- He had a vision in Troas in which a man urged him to go to Macedonia
- He baptized Lydia and her family
- He cast out a spirit of divination out of a soothsayer
- He went back to Ephesus and laid hands on the people, spoke in tongues, prophesied and worked miracles. He used prayer cloths that were used for healing and deliverance.
- Preached in Traos and healed Eutychas by laying on top of him
- An angel appeared to Paul after the ship was sunk by the Euroclydon winds telling him that no life would be lost
- Paul was bitten by a venomous snake in Melita (Malta) and no harm came to him

---

Paul's First Missionary Journey with Barnabas to Cyprus and Asia Minor c AD46-48

http://www.ccel.org/bible/phillips/JBPhillips.htm

Paul's Second Missionary Journey with Silas to Asia Minor and Europe c AD49-52

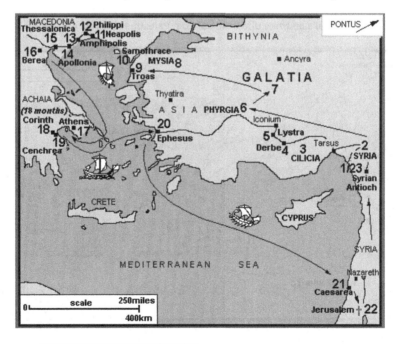

http://www.ccel.org/bible/phillips/JBPhillips.htm

Paul's Third Missionary Journey, returning to Asia Minor and Greece c AD53-58

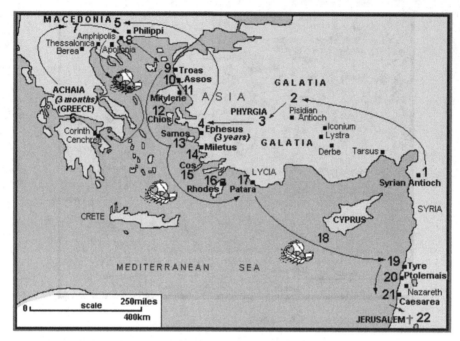

http://www.ccel.org/bible/phillips/JBPhillips.htm

Apostle Paul's Journey under Arrest from Palestine to Rome c AD58-61

http://www.ccel.org/bible/phillips/JBPhillips.htm

SUMMARY QUESTIONS

1. According to the Book of Acts what should happen after the Word of God is preached?

2. How does one receive the Holy Ghost as explained in this book?

3. There is power in testimony. Paul gave his testimony to many in the book of Acts. How did it effect those who heard it?

4. The apostles were persecuted, stoned, imprisoned, and some killed after preaching the Word of God and declaring that Jesus is the son of God. Why do you think they continued to preach the Gospel even when they were mistreated?

5. What type of philosophers, in this present day, are questioning the Word of God and its authenticity?

6. List the different ways God communicated to his people in the book of Acts.

7. What did God communicate to you and how are you going to implement His instructions into your life?

CHAPTER THREE

THE BOOK OF LAMENTATIONS

Step Three: Repent For Your Transgressions

The book of Lamentations is written about Jerusalem as seen through the prophet Jeremiah. Answer the questions as it relates to your life and the society in which you live. These questions are just a guide to help you examine your life in relationship with the most High God. Therefore, write from your human experience.

Chapter 1 – Jerusalem and Sin

1. Describe what happened to Jerusalem in verses 1-4.

2. Why did the Lord afflict her? (5)

3. Are you keeping the Sabbath holy and what does society do on the Sabbath day? (7)

4. What is likely to happen when you let the enemy into your camp/church? (8-11)

5. Who is your enemy? (14)

6. As you fell into sin, did you ever believe that the Lord was angry with you while you experienced the negative consequences of that behavior? (12-14)

7. While in sin did you feel the presence of the Holy Ghost, i.e. the comforter? How has sin effected your children and grandchildren? (16)

8. Have you ever felt alienated from family and friends? Were they available when you needed them? (17-19)

9. Because of life's circumstances, are you feeling the stress anywhere in your body? Describe (20)

10. Are your so-called friends laughing at you and talking behind your back? (21)

11. Are you holding grudges and wishing harm will come to others? (22)

Chapter 2 – Destruction and Judgment

1. At any time in your life have you ever felt a cloud of heaviness over you? (1)

2. Do you believe that at the present time that God is showing his wrath upon the earth? (3)

3. Who or what is being devoured by fire? (3-4)

4. Think about the world in which we live. What nation has been on top and is now falling to its own destruction? What are the other nations of the world saying about this country? (15-16)

5. How should the inhabitants of the land rectify the situation? (19)

6. Are the elders and prophets of the church equipped to handle the problems of today? (10, 14)

7. What has the Lord said about not keeping his commandments? (17)

Chapter 3 – The Soul Condition

1. Read verses 1-17. What was your life like when you turned away from God?

2. Who/What kept you from self-destruction? (20-22)

3. When you were ready to give up your vices, what came from deep within your soul? (24, 55-56)

4. What advantage is there to patiently waiting on God? (25-26, 57-58)

Chapter 4 - Persecution

1. What have you done out of desperation that you would not have done under normal circumstances? (10)

2. When society is lost in sin, who suffers the most? (1:6, 2:11- 12, 19-21)

3. How did the enemy attack your country and were your leaders surprised? (12)

4. Do you believe in your country more than you believe in God? (17)

5. Can you hide your sin from God? (22)

Chapter 5 - Suffering

1. Who have you, or society, sold out to? (1-5)

2. How are we reaping what we have sown? (7)

3. Think about a city where there is high crime and immorality? How are women, children, the poor, and the elderly treated? (9-18)

4. Although the world is deep in sin, do you believe the Lord has forgotten about us? (19-22)

The Lord wants you to stand in the gap and repent for those who are not willing or able to do so. We all have fallen short and sinned. Who has the Lord laid on your heart, your family, employer, city, state, country, government, etc.?

PRAYER OF REPENTANCE

Lord, in the name of Jesus, I repent for the sins committed by my _____. I pray that they will turn from their wicked ways and listen to the voice of the most High God. I pray that they will walk in love, integrity, and honesty. I pray that the Lord will guide them in all their ways and that they look not to their own understanding. In Jesus' name I pray. Amen.

CHAPTER FOUR

𝒯HE BOOK OF GENESIS

Step Four: Forgive Those Who Have Trespassed Against You, God Is A Forgiving God
Genesis is the Greek word for beginning and generations. Genesis will teach you about creation, Adam and Eve, the fall of man, Abraham, Noah, and much more. This is a book about betrayal, sin, covenant promises, faith, hope, and forgiveness. Enjoy this extensive study into the Word of God.

Chapter 1 – The Creation

1. What did God create in the beginning? (1)

2. What was the earth like? (2)

3. Who was moving over the face of the waters? (2)

4. What did God speak into existence and how was it divided? (3-5)

5. Did the first day begin in the morning and end in the evening? (5)

6. What was created in the midst of the waters? (6)

7. What was created on the second day? (8)

8. What was created on the third day? (9-13)

9. What did God create for signs and seasons and for time? (14)

10. Describe the purpose of the greater light and lesser light. What day were they created on? (16-19).

11. What was created on the fifth day? (20-23)

12. What was created on the sixth day? (24-31)

13. What did God create in his own image? (26-27)

14. What dominion was man given and what was his mandate? (26, 28)

Chapter 2 – Man, Woman, And The Garden Of Eden

1. What happened on the seventh day and why did God sanctify that day? (1-3)

2. In the beginning how did the Lord water the earth? (5-6)

3. How did man become a living being and where was he placed? (7-8)

4. What type of trees were in the garden of Eden? (9)

5. What was the Lord's commandment to man (Adam)? (16-17)

6. How were the animals formed and who named them? (19-20)

7. Who was Adam talking about when he said, bone of my bone, flesh of my flesh? (23)

8. How did God create woman (Eve)? (18, 21-22)

9. Who shall be one flesh? (24)

Chapter 3 – The Fall Of Man

1. Describe the serpent and what he said to the woman. (1, 4-5)

2. Was the woman confused about what God said? (2-3)

3. What type of fruit did the first man and woman eat of? (6)

4. Why did the man and woman hide themselves from God? (7, 10)

5. Did the first couple take responsibility for what they did? (12-13)

6. What did God say to the serpent? (14)

7. What consequences did God give Adam and Eve for their disobedience? (16-18, 23)

8. What does Eve mean? (20)

9. Why were the cherubims placed at the east end of the garden? (22, 24)

Chapter 4 – Cain and Abel

1. Who were Adam and Eve's first children and how did they live? (1-2)

2. What did Cain and Abel offer to the Lord? (3-4)

3. What did Cain do to Abel? (8)

4. What were the consequences of this action? (11, 12, 14)

5. How did the Lord react to what Cain did? (9-10)

6. After this where did Cain live? (16)

7. Describe Cain's lineage. (17-23)

8. Who was Seth? (25)

9. When did man begin to call upon the name of the Lord? (26)

Chapter 5 – Adam, Noah, and Lifespan

1. How old was Adam when Seth was born? (3)

2. How long did Adam live? (5)

3. List the ancestors between and Adam and Noah. (5-30)

4. What was the average lifespan? (5-30)

Chapter 6 – The Ark

1. How many years did the Lord promise man? (3)

2. What kind of beings were in the earth then and what did they do? (4)

3. How did God feel about this? (5-7)

4. What did God think about Noah? (8-9)

5. Describe what the earth was like at this time? (11-12)

6. What did God tell Noah? (13)

7. What did God commission Noah to build? (14)

8. What was the purpose of the flood? (17)

9. What did the Lord establish with Noah? (18)

10. What detailed instructions was Noah given by God? (14-16, 19-21)

Chapter 7 – The Flood

1. Summarize the instructions that the Lord gave to Noah? (1-3)

2. How many days of rain did God send upon the earth? (4, 12)

3. How old was Noah when it began to rain? (6)

4. How many days of warning did God give Noah before it started to rain? (4, 10)

5. How many sons did Noah have and did they enter the ark at that time? (7, 13)

6. Who closed up the ark? (16)

7. How long was the earth flooded? (24)

8. Who survived the flood? (21-23)

Chapter 8 – The Waters Recede

1. Describe what God did on the earth in verses 1-3.

2. Where did the ark rest and in what month? (4)

3. How long did it take for the waters to decrease? (5)

4. When it stopped raining, what was the first thing that Noah did? (6-7)

5. How many days did Noah stay in the ark after it stopped raining and why? (10-11)

6. When did Noah remove the covering of the ark? (13)

7. When was the earth completely dry? (14)

8. What did God command Noah to do? (15-17)

9. How did Noah show his reverence for God? (20)

10. What did the Lord promise? (21-22)

Chapter 9 – Covenant and Curse of Canaan

1. What did God tell Noah and his sons? (1-3, 7)

2. What were they forbidden to eat? (4)

3. What does God think about murder? (6)

4. Using your own dictionary, define covenant.

5. What covenant did God make with Noah and his descendants? (9-11)

6. What was the symbol of the covenant? (12-17)

7. Who was Canaan's father? (18)

8. What happened after Noah got drunk? (21)

9. Who did Noah bless and curse? (24-27)

10. How long did Noah live? (28-29)

Chapter 10 – Sons Of Noah

1. What is chapter ten about? (1)

2. Who became a mighty hunter in the earth and what does his name mean? (8-9)

3. Who was born into Japheth's blood line? (2-5)

4. How were the isles of the gentiles divided? (4-5)

5. Who was in Ham's bloodline? (6-20)

6. Describe Shem's bloodline. (21-31)

Chapter 11 – Tower of Babel

1. How many languages were there after the flood? (1)

2. Why were the people in this region able to build a tower that reached into heaven? (6)

3. What did the Lord do after the tower was built? (8-9)

4. Which descendants lived in the region of Babel? (10:8-10)

5. How long did Shem live? (11)

6. Who was in Shem's bloodline? (10-31)

7. Who was Abram's father and brothers? (26-27)

8. Who was Lot's father and where did he die? (27-28)

9. Who did Abram and Nahor marry? (29)

10. Who went to Canaan? (31)

11. How many children did Sarai bear? (30)

Chapter 12 – Abram Leaves His Country

1. Why did the Lord tell Abram to leave his country? (1-3)

2. How old was Abram when he left Horan? (14)

3. Where did the Lord appear to Abram and what did he say? (6-7)

4. Why did Abram go to Egypt? (10)

5. Why did Abram decide to present Sarai as his sister? (11-13)

6. How was Abram treated after entering Pharaoh's house? (16)

7. How did the Lord respond to this? (17)

8. How did Pharaoh respond? (18-20)

Chapter 13 – Abram And Lot

1. Did Abram leave Egypt a poor man? (1-2)

2. Where did Abram call on the name of the Lord? (3-4)

3. Who was in conflict? (7)

4. What was Abram's solution? (9)

5. Where did Lot dwell? (11-12)

6. Where did Abram dwell and what did God promise? (12, 14-17)

7. What kind of people lived in Sodom? (13)

8. Where did Abram settle down and what did he do upon arriving? (18)

Chapter 14 - Melchizedek

1. Which kingdoms were warring against each other and in what region did they reside? (1-3)

2. Who did these nations serve for twelve years and what happened in the thirteenth year? (4)

3. What was Siddim like? (10)

4. What happened to Sodom and Gomorrah and their kings? (10-11)

5. What happened to Lot and what did Abram do about it? (12-16)

6. Who was Melchizedek? (18)

7. Why did Abram refuse to take the merchandise offered by the king of Sodom? (22-23)

Chapter 15 – The Covenant With Abraham

1. What did the Lord say to Abram in a vision? (1, 4, 5, 7)

2. How did Abram respond? (3, 6)

3. Who was Eliezar, how did Abram see him, and how did the Lord respond? (2-4)

4. What was the sacrificial offering for the covenant and how was it performed? (9, 10, 17)

Chapter 16 - Hagar

1. Who was Hagar? (1)

2. How did Abram and Sarai start their family? (2-4)

3. What happened in Abram's household after the child was conceived? (5-6)

4. After Hagar left Abram's household, who found her, and what did he advise? (7-11)

5. How old was Abram when his son was born and what was his name? (11,15,16).

Chapter 17 – Name Change

1. What happened after Abram turned 99 years old? (1-5)

2. After God changed Abram's name what did God promise? (6)

3. Describe the covenant between God and Abram? (7-9)

4. What was the sign of the covenant and when was it to be performed? (10-12)

5. Who else was allowed to have the sign of the covenant? (13)

6. How does God view people who are not circumcised? (14)

7. What name did God change Sarai's name to and what does it mean? (15)

8. Describe her destiny? (16)

9. How did Abraham react to this news? (17)

10. What did the Lord say about Ishmael? (20)

11. What was Abram to name his son and when was he to be born? (19, 21)

12. Explain how Abraham carried out God's orders. (23-27)

Chapter 18 – Angelic Visitation

1. Who appeared to Abraham on the plains of Mamre? (2)

2. What did Abraham and Sarah prepare for their guest? (4-8)

3. What did the visitors tell them? (10)

4. How did they receive the news? (11-14)

5. Where was the Lord headed after his visitation with Abraham and Sarah? (20)

6. How did Abraham try and save the righteous that lived among the wicked? (21-32)

7. What did the Lord decide after they spoke? (32)

Chapter 19 – Sodom and Gomorrah

1. Who met Lot at the gate of Sodom? (1)

2. How did Lot show his hospitality? (3)

3. What did the men of Sodom do? (4-5)

4. What did Lot offer them? (8)

5. Did the men accept it? (9)

6. How did the angels handle this altercation? (10-11)

7. What did the Lord send the angels to do? (13)

8. What did the angels advise Lot to do and how did his relatives respond? (12, 14, 15)

9. The next morning why was Lot and his family hurried out of the city? (15)

10. Where and how was Lot to leave the city? (17)

11. Where did Lot decide to go? (20, 22, 23, 30)

12. How was Sodom and Gomorrah destroyed? (24-25)

13. What happened to Lot's wife? (26)

14. Did Abraham see the destruction of Sodom and Gomorrah? (27-28)

15. What did Lot's daughter's conspire to do? (31-36)

16. Who was Moab and what is his legacy? (37)

17. Who was Benammi and what is his legacy? (38)

Dr. Julia Floyd Jones

Chapter 20 - Abimelech

1. Where did Abraham journey to? (1)

2. What lie did he tell Abimelech about his wife Sarah? (2)

3. How did the king find out about the deception? (3)

4. What did God tell Abimelech to do? (7)

5. How did Abraham justify his actions and perpetuating the lie? (11)

6. How were Abraham and Sarah related before marriage? (12)

7. What gifts did Abraham receive from Abimelech? (14-16)

8. What happened after Abraham prayed for Abimelech? (17-18)

Chapter 21 – Isaac And Ishmael

1. How old was Abraham when his son Isaac was born and what happened on the eighth day? (4-5).

2. Why did Abraham tell Hagar and Ishmael to leave his house and how did he feel about it? (9-11, 14)

3. What did God speak to Abraham about both of his sons? (12-13)

4. When the water was all gone what did Hagar do? 15

5. What happened after God heard the voice of the Lad? (17-19)

6. What skill did Ishmael develop? (20)

7. When Ishmael became of age where did his mother find him a wife? (21)

8. What did Abimelech ask of Abraham? (22-23)

9. What did Abraham give Abimelech as a sign of their covenant? (27, 30, 31)

Chapter 22 – The Sacrifice

1. What did God ask Abraham to do? (2)

2. Who accompanied Abraham and Isaac? (3)

3. What did Isaac say about the burnt offering? (7)

4. Who stopped Abraham from slaying his son? (11-12)

5. What was offered as a burnt offering in the place of Isaac? (13)

6. What did Abraham call the name of that place? (14)

7. What did the Lord tell Abraham about the significance of his obedience? (16-18)

Chapter 23 – Sarah's Death

1. Where did Sarah die and how old was she? (1-2)

2. Explain where Sarah was buried and how much Abraham paid for her burying place? (3-20)

Chapter 24 – Isaac And Rebekah

1. What did Abraham make his servant swear? (2-3, 9)

2. Where did he send the servant? (4, 10)

3. What did the servant prophesy? (14)

4. Who appeared as the servant spoke? (15)

5. What did the servant give Rebekah? (22)

6. Who was Rebekah's brother? (29)

7. After the servant retold his story to Laban, what did he give to the family? (53)

8. Was Rebekah willing to be Isaac's wife? (58, 67)

Chapter 25 – Keturah, Isaac, Ishmael, Esau, And Jacob

1. Abraham married again. What was his second wife's name and who were their children? (1-4)

2. Abraham gave all that he had to Isaac. What did he do with his sons that were born of his concubines? (6)

3. How long did Abraham live? (7)

4. Where did Isaac and Ishmael bury their father? (9-10)

5. Who were Ishmael's descendants? (13-15)

6. How many nations did they represent or govern? (16)

7. How old was Ishmael when he died and where was he buried? (17-18)

8. How old was Isaac when he got married? (20)

9. Rebekah was barren, what happened after Isaac prayed? (21)

10. Describe how Rebekah's children were born. (22-26)

11. What were the boys like when they got older? (27-28)

12. Explain why Esau sold his birth right? (29-34)

Chapter 26 - Abimelech

1. Why did Isaac go to the king of the Philistines? (1)

2. What did the Lord tell Isaac to do? (2-4)

3. What did Isaac do once he arrived in Gerar? (7)

4. Does this sound familiar? Who in his bloodline did this previously?

5. How did the king find out about the deception? (8)

6. What was Isaac's reason for lying? (9)

7. What did Abimelech decree after he heard the truth? (10-11)

8. What did Isaac receive after he sowed in that land and describe his wealth? (12-14)

9. Why did King Abimelech banish Isaac from his kingdom? (16)

10. Where did Isaac set up camp after this? (17)

11. What happened to the wells that were dug by father, Abraham? (15,18, 19)

12. What were the names of the wells? (20-23)

13. What did the Lord say to Isaac? (24)

14. Why did Abimelech seek him out again? (26, 28)

15. What was their covenant about? (29, 31)

16. How old was Esau when he got married and who were his wives? (34)

Chapter 27 – Birth Right

1. What did Isaac tell Esau to do and why? (1-4)

2. What did Rebekah and Jacob conspire to do? (5-10)

3. What was Jacob's fear? (12)

4. How was Jacob disguised to feel and smell like his brother? (15-16)

5. Why did Isaac doubt that he was talking with Esau? (20-22)

6. Why did Isaac decide to give the blessing? (23-27)

7. What was the blessing? (28-29)

8. What happened when Esau came in with his venison? (32-33)

9. How did Esau respond? (34-38)

10. Was he able to retain his birthright? (36-37)

11. What blessing did Esau get from his father? (39-40)

12. What did Esau vow to do to his brother? (41)

13. Who advised Jacob to leave for Horan and why? (42-45)

Chapter 28 – God Speaks To Jacob

1. Why was Jacob told to leave his homeland? (27:46, 28:1-2)

2. Why did Esau visit Ishmael? (8-9)

3. Describe the dream that Jacob had on the way to Haran. (12-15)

4. What did Jacob call the place where he slept and heard from God (19), and what vow did he make unto God? (20-22)

5. Do you believe that God provides all of your needs? Will you give a tenth of your earnings to Him? (20, 22)

Chapter 29 – Jacob Marries and Serves Laban

1. How did Jacob meet his relatives? (1-9)

2. How did Jacob react when he first met Rachel? (10)

3. Jacob lived with Laban and his family one month before they decided on his wages. What did Jacob ask for? (18)

4. What were the names of Laban's daughters? (16)

5. What deception took place between Laban and Jacob? (23-25) How did Laban justify his actions? (26)

6. What was Jacob required to do in order to make Rachel his wife? (27)

7. Although Jacob loved Rachel more than Leah, she was not able to conceive. How did the Lord intervene? (31)

8. What were the names of Jacob and Leah's first four sons? Did her child bearing capability give her favor with Jacob? (32-35)

Chapter 30 – Jacob's Children

1. What was Rachel's ultimatum to Jacob? (1)

2. What does the fruit of the womb mean? (2)

3. Why was Jacob given Bilhal? (3)

4. How many sons did Bilhal bear? (5, 6, 8)

5. In retaliation Leah gave her maid to Jacob to conceive more of his children. How many children did Zilpah have for Jacob? (11, 13)

6. Leah and Jacob had more children together, name them. (18, 20)

7. What was the name of the son that Rachel conceived with Jacob? (25)

8. When Jacob had his first son with Rachel, what did he ask Laban? (25-26)

9. How were the cattle, sheep, and goats, divided among Laban and Jacob? (32-43)

Chapter 31 – Jacob Leaves Laban

1. What did Laban's sons say about Jacob? (1)

2. When Jacob noticed Laban's change in attitude, what did he decide to do? (3-4)

3. What did Jacob say about his father-in-law? (6-7)

4. How did God intervene to increase Jacob's wealth? (9-12)

5. How did God identify himself? (13)

6. What objects did Rachel take from her father? (19)

7. When did Laban find out about Jacob's departure? (22)

8. On the seventh day, what did God tell Laban in a dream? (24)

9. What did Laban say to Jacob when they met face-to-face? (26-30)

10. What did Laban search for in the tents? (30-33)

11. Where were they hidden? (34-35)

What is hidden in your home or car that needs to be disposed of? If you do not know ask the Holy Spirit to reveal it to you.

12. How long did Jacob work for Laban? (38)

13. Describe the covenant between Jacob and Laban. (50)

14. What did they call the altar? (47-48)

15. Did Laban come to terms with his daughters departing with Jacob to return to his homeland? (55)

Chapter 32 – Jacob And Esau Prepare To Meet, Jacob Wrestles With An Angel

1. Who did Jacob meet while traveling? (1)

2. What is Mahanaim? (2)

3. What did Jacob command his servants to tell Esau? (4-5)

4. How did Esau receive the news? (6)

5. What did Jacob expect after this? (7-11)

6. How did Jacob plan for Esau's supposed retaliation? (16-20)

7. What happened after Jacob sent his family ahead and he was left alone? (24)

8. How did Jacob's hip get out of socket? (25-26)

9. What did Jacob want from the "man"? (26)

10. Why did God change Jacob's name to Israel? What does it mean? (28)

11. Who did Jacob believe he was wrestling with and did he receive his blessing? (29-30)

12. What does Peniel mean? (30)

13. Describe the tradition that was started by the children of Israel because of Jacob's experience at Peniel? (32)

Chapter 33 - Reconciliation

1. Describe the meeting between Jacob and Esau. (1-7)

2. Why didn't Jacob return to his homeland with Esau immediately after they met? (13-14)

3. Name the places that Jacob camped at during his journey. (17-18)

4. He erected an altar where he bought land from Shecham. What did he call it and what does it mean? (20)

Chapter 34 – Dinah Is Violated

1. What happened to Dinah, Leah, and Jacob's daughter? (1-2)

2. How did the men of Dinah's family react to this? (5, 7)

3. What did Hamor ask of Jacob? (8-12)

4. How did Jacob's sons respond? (14-18)

5. What happened on the third day after the men were circumcised? (25-29)

6. What did Jacob say to Simeon and Levi? (30)

Chapter 35 – The Death Of Rachel And Isaac

1. What did the Lord instruct Jacob to do? (1)

2. Were Jacob's relatives worshiping false gods? (2)

3. What did Jacob do with the idols? (4)

4. What did Jacob call the place in Bethel where he built the altar? (7)

5. What did God tell Jacob when he appeared to him again in Padanaram? (10-12)

6. What happened to Rachel during childbirth? (16)

7. What did Rachel and Jacob name this child? (18)

8. Where was Rachel buried? (19)

9. How many sons did Jacob have? Name them: (23-26)

10. Jacob finally made it back to his homeland to see his father. How long did Isaac live and where was he buried? (27-29)

Chapter 36 – The Descendants of Esau

1. This chapter explains the genealogy of Esau. Who were his wives? (2)

2. Where did Esau move and why? (6-9)

3. Who were Esau's sons? (10)

4. What is significant about the Kings of Edom? (31)

5. Who were the dukes or chiefs of Edom? (40-43)

6. What nation did Esau birth? (43)

Chapter 37 - Joseph

1. Where did Jacob take up residence? (1)

2. How old was Joseph at the beginning of this chapter and why was he is father's favorite child? (2-3)

3. What did Jacob make for Joseph? (3)

4. How did Joseph's brothers react to him as the favorite child? (4)

5. Describe Joseph's dreams and how his family reacted to them? (5-10)

6. What happened to Joseph after his father sent him to Shecham to check on his brothers? (13-24)

7. Which brother kept Joseph from being killed? (21-22)

8. What did Judah suggest that they do with Joseph? (27)

9. Where was Joseph taken and how much was he sold for? (28, 36)

10. Was Reuben in the plan to sell Joseph? (29-30)

11. How did the brothers convince their father that Joseph was dead? (31-32)

12. How did Jacob react to this news? (34-35)

Chapter 38 – Judah And Tamar

1. Who did Judah conceive three children with? (2-5)

2. What were the names of his sons that he conceived with her? (3-5)

3. Who was Tamar? (6)

4. What happened to Er and Onan? (7-10)

5. What did Judah tell Tamar to do? (11)

6. Did Judah keep his word? (14)

7. What did Tamar do in retaliation? (14-18)

8. What happened when Judah sent his payment for services to the harlot? (20-22)

9. When did Judah find out about Tamar and what was the outcome? (24-26)

10. Describe what happened after the birth of the twins. (27-30)

Chapter 39 – Joseph In Egypt
1. Where was Joseph taken? (1)

2. How was it known that the Lord was with Joseph? (2, 3)

3. What did Potiphar think of Joseph? (4-6)

4. What happened after Joseph refused to sleep with Potiphar's wife? (7-20)

5. How did Joseph prosper in prison? (21-23)

Chapter 40 – Interpretation Of Dreams
1. Why did Pharaoh's chief butler and chief baker end up in prison? (1-2)

2. Who was put in charge of them? (3-4)

3. Through what source should dream interpretation take place? (8)

4. Briefly summarize the chief butler's dream. (9-11)

5. What was the interpretation of the dream that the Lord gave Joseph? (12-13)

6. What did Joseph ask the butler in return for the interpretation of his dream? (14)

7. Describe the chief baker's dream? (16-17)

8. How did Joseph interpret the dream? (18-19)

9. When did the dreams come to pass and did the chief butler honor Joseph's request? (20-23)

Chapter 41 – Pharaoh's Dreams

1. What happened two years later? (1)

2. How many dreams did Pharaoh have and who did he call to interpret his dreams and were they able to do so? (2-8)

3. What did the chief butler say at this point? (9-13)

4. Who did Pharaoh call next to interpret his dream? (14)

5. Did Joseph take credit for dream interpretation? (16, 28)

6. What was the interpretation of the dream? (25-31)

7. Why did God allow Pharaoh the opportunity about what was about to take place in two different dreams? (32)

8. Explain how Joseph planned to circumvent the famine. (33-36)

9. Describe how Pharaoh promoted Joseph. (40-44)

10. What was Joseph's Egyptian name and who did he marry? (45)

11. How old was Joseph when he received this promotion? (46)

12. Joseph had two sons before the famine. What were the meanings of their names? (51-52)

13. The famine effected the entire region. Was Joseph able to feed the people from other areas as well as the Egyptians? (54-57)

Chapter 42 – Joseph's Brothers

1. Where did Jacob send 10 of his sons to buy corn? (1-2)

2. Why was the youngest named Benjamin, left behind? (4)

3. When Jacob's sons arrived in Egypt did they recognize their brother Joseph? (7-8)

4. What posture did Joseph's brothers take when they saw him? Was this symbolic of the dream Joseph had as a child? (6, 9)

5. Reuben said something that brought Joseph to tears, explain. (22-24)

6. Which brother was held as ransom to ensure that the others returned with Benjamin? (24)

7. What did Joseph restore to his brothers? (25)

8. How did Jacob feel about the demands that were made on the family? (35-38)

Chapter 43 – Brothers Return With Benjamin

1. Did Jacob's sons return to Egypt soon after they got back home? (2, 10)

2. Jacob was exasperated because his sons told Joseph so much about their family. What did he instruct his sons to take back to Egypt? (11-13)

3. How did Joseph greet them? (15-26)

4. How did Joseph react when he saw his youngest brother? (29-31)

5. What is an abomination to the Egyptians? (32)

6. In spite of the social class differences, did they have a good time? (34)

Chapter 44 – Joseph Tests His Brothers

1. What did Joseph conspire against his brother? (1-6)

2. In anguish, what did Judah tell Joseph about the family situation? (16-30)

3. What did Judah expect to happen to his father if he did not return home with Benjamin? (31-34)

Chapter 45 – Joseph Reveals His Identity

1. Why did Joseph tell his servants to leave his presence? (1-4)

2. What was the plan and purpose for Joseph's life? (7-8)

3. Because there were five years left in the famine, where did Joseph tell his brothers to dwell? (10-11)

4. What message did Joseph send his father via his brothers? (9, 13)

5. How did Pharaoh respond to this news? (16-20)

6. Joseph gave all of his brothers a change of clothes, what else did he give Benjamin? (22)

7. What provisions did Joseph send his father? (23)

8. What did Jacob want to do before he died? (28)

Chapter 46 – Jacob Moves To Egypt

1. Where did God speak to Jacob and what was the message? (1-4)

2. How many of Jacob's biological relatives followed him to Egypt? (26)

3. Where did Joseph and Jacob meet? (28)

4. Why did Joseph tell his brothers to lie about their profession? (34)

5. Why did Jacob believe that he could now die in peace? (30)

Chapter 47 – Jacob Meets Pharaoh, Famine In The Land

1. When Pharaoh asked Joseph's brothers what they did for a living how did they respond? (3)

2. Did Pharaoh respond negatively? (6)

3. How old was Jacob when he met Pharaoh? (9)

4. How did the famine increase Pharaoh's wealth? (14-20)

5. Where did he relocate the people? (21)

6. Who was exempt from the move? (22)

7. When the common people were no longer able to pay for food, how did Joseph sustain them? (23-26)

8. How long did Jacob live in Egypt? (28)

9. Where did Jacob want to be buried? How did Joseph honor his father's wishes? (29, 31)

Chapter 48 – Ephraim And Manasseh

1. When Joseph heard that his father was sick he went to visit him with his sons. What did Jacob tell him? (3-4)

2. Were Ephraim and Manasseh included in the inheritance of Abraham, Isaac, and Jacob? (5)

3. According to Hebrew tradition who was supposed to receive the blessing? (18)

4. How did Jacob bless Joseph's sons? (14, 16, 20)

5. What did Joseph say to his father when he put his right hand on Ephraim's head? (17-18)

6. Did his father know what he was doing, explain? (19)

7. How did Jacob (Israel) bless Joseph? (21-26)

Chapter 49 – Jacob Prophesies Over His Sons

1. Jacob gathered his son together and spoke prophetic words over each of them, explain. (1-27)

2. Where did he tell his sons to bury him? (29-30)

3. What happened to Jacob after he finished this decree? (33)

Chapter 50 – Death And Mourning

1. Jacob was embalmed according to Egyptian tradition. How long was the process? (1-3)

2. How long did Joseph and the Egyptians mourn? (3)

3. Who went with Joseph to bury his father? (7-9)

4. Where did the seven days of mourning take place? (10)

5. How did the Canaanites respond? (11)

6. What were Joseph's brothers worried about? (15)

7. How did Joseph respond? (19-21)

8. How many generations of Ephraim's children were birthed before Joseph died? (23)

9. Where did Joseph live, die, and get buried? (22, 26)

10. What did Joseph decree unto his brethren? (24)

COMPARATIVE SUMMARY

The following summary will help you to retain what you have studied in the book of Genesis. You will be able to see the family patterns both negatively and positively and the impact of them throughout the generations. God is a forgiving God. He overlooks our sins and imperfections so that His plan will be accomplished in the earth.

COVENANTS

Noahic Covenant

The Lord promised that he would never create another flood to destroy the earth. This covenant was between Noah and his descendants and all of the animals that were in the ark. God chose the rainbow as his symbol of the covenant (Genesis (9:1-18).

Abrahamic Covenant

The Lord told Abram that he would be the father of many nations, not only in offspring but in land. Circumcision was the sign of the covenant. God changed Abrams name to Abraham and Sarai's name to Sarah (Genesis 15:1-21, 17:1-14).

Abraham and Abimelech

The covenant was established to preserve peace so that the inhabitants of the land would not fight over a well at Beersheba (Genesis 21:22-34).

Abimelech and Isaac

Abimelech established another covenant at Beersheba with Isaac to preserve peace over disputed water well rights (Genesis 26:26-31).

Laban and Jacob (31:43-53)

Jacob agreed not to take any other wives besides the daughters of Laban. Jacob and Laban agreed not to invade each other's territories when Jacob left to return to Canaan (Genesis 31: 43-53).

BETRAYAL AND DECEPTIONS

Cain and Abel

Cain killed his brother Abel. God punishes Cain by causing him to wander throughout the land and as a farmer he will no longer yield productive crops (Genesis 4: 8-9).

Abram, Sarai, and Pharaoh

Abram deceived Pharaoh and said that Sarai was his sister so that he would not be killed. Even though they were half-siblings he failed to mention they were married. Pharaoh and his house were hit by plagues because of the deception (Genesis 12: 10-20).

Lot and His Daughters

Some men of Sodom come to Lot's house looking for his male guests to have sex with them. Lot offers them his virgin daughters instead, but the men refuse. Lot and his daughters left Sodom before it was destroyed by the wrath of God and they lived in a cave for a period of time. Lot's daughters were isolated from other men and wanted to carry on the family lineage. They decided to each bear their father's child without his consent by getting him drunk (Genesis 19:8, 31-36).

Abraham, Sarah, and Abimelech

Abraham lied again about Sarah being his sister. The Lord spoke to Abimelech in a dream and told him of the deception (Genesis 20: 11-18).

Isaac, Rachel, and Abimelech

Isaac perpetuated the same lie as his father before him. He told Abimelech and the other men of that region that Rachel was his sister. He thought this was going to preserve his life (Genesis 26: 2-17).

Esau and Jacob

Esau sells Jacob his birthright as firstborn, for a bowel of stew. Rebekah and Jacob successfully conspire against Esau to withhold his blessing as firstborn, given by his father, Isaac (Genesis 25:30-34, 27:1-40).

Laban and Jacob

Laban deceived Jacob and gave his daughter Leah to be Jacob's first wife instead of Rachel who he loved. Laban continued to be very deceitful and changed Jacob's wages ten times in a twenty year period. Laban tried to cheat Jacob out of his share of the livestock (Genesis 29:23-26, 30:25-43).

Joseph and His Brothers

Joseph's brothers conspired to kill him because he was favored by their father. Instead of killing him they sold him into slavery. They told their father Jacob (Israel), that Joseph had been killed by a wild animal (Genesis 37:13-36).

Tamar and Judah

Tamar was Er's wife. Er was the son of Judah who was killed by the Lord because of his wickedness. Judah promised Tamar that when his youngest son, Shelah, became of age that he would allow him to marry her. When that did not happen Tamar took things into her own hands and conceived twins with her father-in-law, Judah, through deceit (Genesis 38:11-26).

Joseph and Potifer's Wife

Potifer's wife wanted Joseph to have sex with her. When he refused her repeated advances she took revenge. She told Potifer, her husband, that Joseph tried to have sex with her. Joseph was put in prison for a crime he did not commit (Genesis 39:7-20).

BLESSINGS

In biblical history, blessings were prayers spoken over children and grandchildren that were prophetic in nature. Once spoken, they could not be taken back.

Isaac

Isaac receives the blessing of the Abrahamic covenant through birth, *for in Isaac shall thy seed be called, and in thy seed shall all the nations of the earth be blessed (Genesis 22: 12, 18).*

Ishmael

Ishmael was the first born of Abraham's son but not through his wife Sarah, therefore he did not receive the covenant blessing. However, God the Father blessed him and his descendants, *of the son of the bondwoman will I make a nation because he is thy seed (Genesis 21:13).*

Esau

Even though Esau did not receive the blessing of the first-born, his father Isaac still spoke a blessing over him. *Behold thy dwelling shall be the fatness of the earth and of the dew of heaven from above. By the sword shalt thou live and shalt serve thy brother. It will come to pass when thou shalt have dominion that thou shalt break his yoke from off thy neck (Genesis 27:39–40).*

HISTORY OF EDOM

The Lord wants you to understand who Esau was and how his rebellious nature effected several generations. This brief history of Esau and his descendants, the Edomites, is taken from thirteen books of the Bible which confirms their influence in biblical history.

Esau was the firstborn of the twins, Esau and Jacob, but he sold his birthright for a bowl of stew. He not only sells it but also swears and oath to Jacob. He did not understand or respect the spiritual significance of the birthright or of speaking an oath. Esau treated something sacred as common. Jacob took advantage of his twin's blatant disregard for God's blessing and spiritual law. Jacob so understood the power of the blessing that he and his mother were successful in fooling Isaac into giving Jacob the blessing of the first-born son. When Esau became aware that he lost the blessing, twice, he tearfully tried to regain it without repentance for his transgression with God and his earthly father (Genesis 25:30-34, Hebrews 12:16-17).

Genesis 27 describes Esau as a man of the fields. It is my opinion that he spent a lot of time in the fields away from his family and was influenced by other cultures and spiritual forces that allowed him to make light of his culture's traditions. When he turned forty, Esau married two Hittite women, which displeased his mother Rebekah. They were not of his ethnic line and were considered heathens by the Hebrews (Genesis 26:34).

Later, Esau goes to visit his uncle Ishmael, and marries one of his daughters. Isn't it ironic that he marries into the line of another first born son who did not receive the birthright (Genesis 36:1-4).

Esau and his descendants lived on Mt. Seir which was later called Edom and his descendants were called Edomites. Mt. Seir was given to Esau by God and his heritage was said to be given to the dragons of the wilderness. It was a desolate land full of jackals. Mt Seir was also called the territory of wickedness by God. For a while, Edom made the desolate place great (Malachi 1:1-2; Deuteronomy 2:4-5). When the Israelites were wandering in the desert, the Edomites refused to let them pass through their land and threatened to war against them if they did (Numbers 20:20-21). Even though Jacob and Esau reconciled in their later years, what Esau spoke earlier about hating his brother and slaying him, came to pass and is recorded throughout the history of their generations (Genesis 27:41).

Edom did not inherit the birthright as the first born, but they were first to institute a monarchy to rule over their people before Israel had kings. Genesis 36:31 – 39 lists the names of their first kings. The first king Bela (destruction), son of Beor (burning), lived in the city of Dinahabah (give thou judgment). When the names are translated, as shown in parentheses, it gives a brief history of Edom. Heed the warning, what you call yourself, who you socialize with, and where you live are important. Names have power in the spirit realm.

Later in biblical history Saul conquers Edom as written in I Samuel 14:47. Then David conquers Edom and kills all the males and establishes a military post there (2 Samuel 8:14, I Kings 11:15-16). It is also written that Edom revolted against Judah and ten thousand were killed in Edom. Their name was changed to Joktheel which means the blessedness of God (2 Kings 14:7; 8:20-22). Edom and Esau means red. So the people went from being called red to blessed. Which one would you choose?

Ezekiel prophesied that the Lord would take vengeance on Edom because it warred against Judah. The Lord promised to cut off man and beast from Edom and to make it desolate. Ezekiel prophesied against Mt. Seir for it to become desolate and for the men to die by the sword (Ezekiel 25:12-14, 35:2), and it eventually happened. This was also spoken by Isaac over Esau as his blessing.

The Lord said Jacob have I loved and Esau have I hated (Romans 9:13) and He continues to release punishment upon Edom (Amos 1:11). The one chapter book of Obadiah describes the betrayal of Edom against Judah (Israel), the descendants of the twins warring against each other. The Edomites often boasted over their conquest of Judah but the Lord punished them through annihilation. In the end, Judah conquered Edom, and Judah was triumphant. It may not happen in your lifetime, but what God promises will come to pass.

Jacob

Even though Jacob was not the first-born, he was able to receive the blessing that should have been given to his older brother Esau. *Therefore God give thee of the dew of heaven and the fatness of the earth and plenty of corn and wine. Let people serve thee, and nations bow down to thee, be lord over thy brethren and let thy mother's sons bow down to thee. Cursed be everyone that curseth thee, and blessed be he that blesseth thee (Genesis 27:28, 29).*

Jacob received another blessing from the Lord after he wrestled with Him all night. The Lord changed his name from Jacob to Israel (Genesis 32:24-28).

Joseph's Dreams

The blessing that Isaac spoke over Jacob is similar to the dream that Joseph had in his youth.

For behold we were binding sheaves in the field and lo my sheaf arose and also stood upright and behold your sheaves stood around about and made obeisance to my sheaf. Behold I have dreamed a dream more and behold the sun and moon and the eleven stars made obeisance to me (37:7,9). And he told it to his father and to his brethren and his father rebuked him and said unto him, what is this dream that thou hast dreamed? Shall I and thy mother and thy brethren indeed come to bow down ourselves to thee to the earth (37:10)? This was a prophetic dream given to Joseph by the Lord. Because of the events that were about to ensue in Joseph's life and his divine purpose, his destiny had to be spoken. Amos 3:7 states *surely the Lord God will do nothing, but he revealeth his secret unto his servants the prophets.*

Manasseh and Ephraim

Before Jacob's death, he blessed his grandsons Manasseh and Ephraim. Jacob blessed the youngest son, Ephraim with his right hand, giving him the birthright of an eldest son (Genesis 48:12-19).

TWINS

Look at the similarities in the birth of Esau and Jacob and Tamar's twins Pharez and Zarah. The color red has both positive and negative connotations but in the scriptures with the twins, red symbolizes; sin, death, war, and bloodshed. This is evident in the history of Esau's descendants which is included in the previous section.

Esau and Jacob

And the Lord said unto her, two nations are in thy womb and two manner of people shall be stronger than the other people and the elder shall serve the younger. And when her days to be delivered were fulfilled there were twins in her womb. And the first came out red all over like a hairy garment and they called his name Esau. And after that came his brother out and his hand took hold on Esau's heel and his name was called Jacob (Genesis 25: 23-26).

Pharez and Zarah

And it came to pass in the time of her travail that behold twins were in her womb. And it came to pass when she travailed that the one put out his hand and the midwife took and bound upon his hand a scarlet thread, saying, this came out first. And it came to pass as he drew back his hand that behold his brother came out, and she said how has thou broken forth? This breach be upon thee therefore his name was called Pharez. And afterward came out his brother that had the scarlet thread upon his hand and his name was called Zarah (Genesis 38:27–30).

In this study it is important to understand that birth order is important to God and that His kingdom principles are not to be taken lightly. Violating God's statues have consequences and the ability to effect several generations. They must be obeyed whether or not you have come into the understanding of them or not. You must trust God and His Word to be true.

Kingdom principles have been lost in Western society and must be reestablished if Christians are to rule and reign with Christ. Ignorance will not release you of the responsibility but it will cause you to perish and to be consumed by the powers of darkness.

Parents have the ability to bless or curse their children as written in God's Word. God put power in the spoken word that includes blessings and curses. Inheritance and birth order are important, don't take it lightly like Esau. It is never too late to bless your children. Pray about what God wants you to speak over them and watch their lives change for the better.

When Isaac and Jacob blessed their children, their words were prophetic in nature. What they spoke over their children came to pass. In those days, the names of the children were important because you became what you were called. That spiritual law still holds true today. In our studies we read where the Lord changed Abram's, Sarai's, and Jacob's names in order for them to become what they were called and to fulfill their destiny.

Abraham, Isaac, Jacob, and Joseph spoke blessings over their offspring so that God's purpose would be established in the earth. In Genesis chapter 49, Jacob prophesied over his sons before he died, and it came to pass.

Another principle to remember is that the life is in the blood and the blood will cry out as with Cain and Abel. When you shed someone else's blood, take an oath or sign a contract in blood, then you have cursed yourself and delivered your soul into the kingdom of darkness.

What good is it if you gain the world and lose your soul (Mark 8:36) for fifteen minutes of fame on a reality show, a fleeting record contract, or the promises of being a top model. Heed the warning and do not sell your birthright as a Christian, a king and a priest, under the new covenant. If you are guilty of selling out, repent before the Lord and ask for forgiveness. If you have not done so, it will be necessary for you to work step 6 in the handbook, *12 Steps To Overcoming Tragic Life Events*. Trust in the Lord, He will set you free.

TRANSFERENCE OF WEALTH
Abram and Sarai

When Abram lived in Egypt Pharaoh gave him livestock and servants while Sarai lived in the palace with Pharaoh. When Abram, Lot, and Sarai left Egypt they were given livestock as well as silver and gold (Genesis 12:13, 13:1-2). When Abraham and Sarah lived in Ambimelech's kingdom he also gave them livestock and silver (Genesis 20).

Isaac and Rebekah

When Isaac and Rebekah lived in the land of Ambimelech's, Isaac received a hundredfold return on what he sowed. He was also rich with livestock and servants (Genesis 26:9-16).

The Hebrews and the Exodus

The Lord instructed the Hebrews to borrow jewels of silver and of gold from the Egyptians before they left Egypt (Exodus 11:2, 12:35**).**

Jesus and the Wise Men

When Jesus was born wise men from the east presented Him with gold, frankincense, and myrrh (Matthew 2:11). In that era, all three were precious commodities.

SIGNIFICANCE OF THE NUMBER FORTY

The number forty is used to signify purification and spiritual preparedness through trials. The process is designated for a specified period of time i.e. forty days or forty years (Price, 2006). The following examples are found in the books of Genesis, Exodus, Numbers, Matthew, and Acts. God prepared the following people in order for them to fulfill their destiny.

Noah

- The Lord sent rain for forty days and forty nights to flood the earth (Gen. 7:4).
- Noah opened the window of the ark forty days after the rained stopped (Gen. 8:6).

Moses

- The Hebrews spent forty times ten years (400) as slaves in Egypt before Moses delivered them (Exodus 12:40).
- Moses spent his first forty years living in Egyptian royalty as a possible heir to the throne (Exodus 2:1-14, Acts 7:23).
- Moses spends his second forty years in Midian with his wife, children, and in-laws (Exodus 2:15-25).
- Moses was eighty when he returned to Egypt as the deliverer of the Hebrew people and spends his last forty years among them (Exodus 7:7, Deuteronomy 34:7)

- Moses communed with the Lord on Mt. Sinai for forty days and forty nights (Exodus 24:18).
- The Hebrews spent forty years wandering in the wilderness (Numbers 14:33).
- The Hebrews ate manna for forty years (Exodus 16:35).

Joseph
- When Jacob died, Joseph had him embalmed according to Egyptian tradition which took forty days. The Egyptians also mourned with Joseph for forty days (Genesis 50:2-3).

Jesus
- Jesus fasted and spent forty days and forty nights in the wilderness to be tempted of the devil (Matthew 4:1-2).
- Jesus spent forty days on earth after his resurrection (Acts 1:3).

SUMMARY QUESTIONS
1. How much time have you spent in the wilderness?

2. Is your journey complete and what was the purpose?

3. Explain your spiritual development during this process.

4. What did God reveal to you during this time?

CHAPTER FIVE

$\mathcal{T}$HE BOOK OF PSALMS

Step Five: Pray Without Ceasing The Word Of God Shall Continually Be In Thy Mouth

The Book of Psalms is a book of songs and a book of prayers. It is a very lengthy and a very diverse book of scriptures. There are six authors in the Book of Psalms which are as follows: Moses wrote Psalm 90, David wrote 73 Psalms, Asaph wrote Psalms 50, and Psalms 73-83. Historians believe that Solomon wrote Psalms 72 and 127. Heman wrote Psalm 88 and Ethan wrote Psalm 89. Twelve psalms are said to be written by the Sons of Korah, and sixty one Psalms are anonymous.

The Book of Psalms is also arranged into five books. Book I consist of Psalms 1-41, Book II consists of Psalms 42-72, Book III contains Psalms 73-89, Book IV contains Psalm 90-106, and Book V is comprised of Psalms 107-150. The Psalms can be categorized by subject matter as well. For instance there are Psalms of wisdom, confidence, and Psalms of lament, etc.

Your assignment is to read the book in its entirety and highlight the chapters or verses that speak to your heart. Taylor the verses by grouping them in your own order, put music to them, and pray them. Let the Spirit lead. If your prayer life needs a jump start use the book of Psalms. It contains verses that will fit any situation.

I suggest that you use a study Bible for this assignment. It will help you to organize your thoughts. Ask the Lord what is to be your focus of study and look up the verses or books that correspond with what the Lord has told you.

Focus of study_____

Books and verses _____

The following Psalms chosen for this section were given subtitles and some verses were rearranged for my personal expression. This is just an example. Be sure to follow what the Lord has told you to do.

Psalm 33, All Nations Under God

Blessed is the nation whose God is the Lord and the people he hath chosen for his own inheritance(12). Let thy mercy, O Lord, be upon us according as we hope in thee (22). From the place of his habitation he looketh upon all the inhabitants of the earth (14). The Lord looketh from heaven he beholdeth all the sons of men (13). The counsel of the Lord standeth forever, the thoughts of his heart to all generations (11). The Lord bringeth the counsel of the heathen to nought, he maketh devices of the people of none effect (10). Let all the earth fear the Lord, let all the inhabitants of the world stand in awe of him (8). Blessed is the nation whose God is the Lord and the people whom he hath chosen for his own inheritance (12). Let thy mercy, O Lord, be upon us according as we hope in thee (22).

Psalm 103, The Lord Blesses Me

Bless the Lord, O my soul and all that is within me, bless his holy name. Bless the Lord O my soul, and forget not all his benefits, who forgiveth all thine iniquities who healeth all thy diseases, who redeemeth thy life from destruction, who crowneth thee with loving kindness and tender mercies, who satisfieth thy mouth with good things so that thy youth is renewed like the eagle's (1-5).

Psalm 100, How To Come Into The Presences Of The Lord

Make a joyful noise unto the Lord all ye lands. Serve the Lord with gladness, come before his presence with singing. Know ye that the Lord he is God, it is he that hath made us and not we ourselves, we are his people and the sheep of his pasture. Enter into his gates with thanksgiving and into his courts with praise, be thankful unto him and bless his name. For the Lord is good, his mercy is everlasting, and his truth endureth to all generations (1-5).

Psalm 23, God Never Leaves Me Nor Forsakes Me

The Lord is my shepherd, I shall not want. He maketh me to lie down in green pastures, he leadeth me beside still waters. He restoreth my soul. He leadeth me in the paths of righteousness for his name's sake. Yea, though I walk through the valley of the shadow of death, I will fear no evil for thou art with me, thy rod and thy staff they comfort me. Thou preparest a table before me in the presence of mine enemies thou anoinest my head with oil, my cup runneth over. Surely goodness and mercy shall follow me all the days of my life and I will dwell in the house of the Lord forever (1-6).

Psalm 91, The Lord Is My Refuge And My Fortress

He that dwelleth in the secret place of the most high shall abide under the shadow of the Almighty. I will say of the Lord, He is my refuge and my fortress my God in him will I trust. Surely he shall deliver thee from the snare of the fowler, and from the noisome pestilence. He shall cover thee with his feathers, and under his wings shalt thou trust, his truth shall be thy shield and buckler. Thou shall not be afraid for the terror by night nor for the arrow that flieth by day. Nor for the pestilence that walketh in darkness, nor for the destruction that wasteth at noonday, a thousand shall fall at thy side, and ten thousand at thy right hand but it shall not come nigh thee. Only with thine eyes shalt thou behold and see the reward of the wicked. Because thou has made the Lord which is my refuge even the most High thy habitation, there shall no evil befall thee, neither shall any plague come nigh thy dwelling. For he shall give his angels charge over thee to keep thee in all thy ways. They shall bear thee up in their hands lest thou dash thy foot against a stone. Thou shalt tread upon the lion and adder, the young lion and the dragon shalt thou trample under feet. Because he has set his love upon me therefore will I deliver him, I will set him on high because he hath known my name. He shall call upon me and I will answer him, I will be with him in trouble I will deliver him and honor him. With long life will I satisfy him and show him my salvation (1-16).

Now it is your turn to study the Psalms assigned to you by the Holy Spirit. Write them down in your journal.

What did you learn from the study?

CHAPTER SIX

$\mathcal{T}$HE BOOK OF EXODUS

Step Six: Deliverance From Strongholds

Exodus is also called the second book of Moses and explains Hebrew custom, the exodus of the Hebrews out of Egypt and slavery, the plagues, the parting of the Red Sea, the covenant, the tabernacle, the priesthood, and much more. Take your time in this study because there are forty power-packed chapters that will change your life.

Chapter 1 - Egypt

1. How many of Jacob's relatives followed him to Egypt? (5)

2. Why were the Hebrews put into bondage? (7-10)

3. Did the Hebrew population diminish due to the harsh living conditions? (12)

4. How did the Pharaoh attempt to control the burgeoning population? (16, 22)

Chapter 2 - Moses

1. What happened when Pharaoh's daughter came down to the river? (5-9)

2. What did Pharaoh's daughter call her adopted son? (10)

3. What did Moses do as an adult that caused him to flee to Midian? (11-15)

4. How did Moses help the women at the well and who were they? (16-17)

5. Who did Moses marry? What was the name of his wife and first born? (21-22)

6. In the meantime what was happening in Egypt? (23)

7. How did God react? (24-25)

Chapter 3 – The Call

1. What kind of experience did Moses have while he was on the backside of the desert? (1-2)

2. How many times did God call Moses and what instructions were given about his shoes? (4-5)

3. How did the Lord identify himself? (5-6)

4. Why was the Lord sending Moses back to Egypt? (7-10)

5. How did Moses express his lack of confidence? (11, 13)

6. What name of God was Moses supposed to use? (14)

7. What else did God tell Moses to say? (15-17)

8. Because of the mandate what was to come of the Hebrew people? (18-22)

Chapter 4 – Instruction, Insecurity, And Return

1. Moses did not believe that the Hebrews would listen to him. Explain how the Lord was going to get their attention? (2-9)

2. Moses had a speech impediment. What did the Lord say about this defect? (11-16)

3. What object was chosen to show signs and wonders? (17)

4. What did Moses ask of his father-in-law? (18)

5. What happened to the men in Midian that wanted to kill Moses? (19)

6. Moses returned to Egypt with his wife and son. What did God instruct him to say to Pharoah? (22-23)

7. What did his wife Zopporah do? (22-23)

8. What happened after Aaron and Moses met? (27-29)

9. How did the Hebrews react? (31)

Chapter 5 – Meeting With Pharaoh

1. Moses told Pharaoh to let his people go. How did Pharaoh respond? (2)

2. What type of retaliation did Pharaoh impose on the Hebrews because of the demands placed on him by Moses and Aaron? (7-9)

3. What was Pharaoh's reasoning for the increased labor? (8, 17)

4. How did Pharaoh punish the Hebrews for complaining again? (19)

5. What did Moses say to the Lord after this series of punishments? (23)

Chapter 6 – The Covenant And The Generations

1. How did the Lord identify himself in these verses? (2-3)

2. What land was given to the Hebrews as part of the covenant? (4)

3. What did the Lord say that he would do concerning the Hebrews? (5-8)

4. What did the Lord tell Moses to do after the children of Israel refused to listen to him? (11)

5. Who did the Lord tell Moses to speak to within the Hebrew tribe? (14-25)

6. Describe Moses' and Aaron's parents and the tribes they came from. (19-20)

7. How many children did Aaron have by Elisheba? (23)

8. What did Moses mean when he said he had uncircumcised lips? (12, 30)

Chapter 7 – The Plague of Blood

1. What did God say to Moses and Aaron? (1-2)

2. Why did God harden Pharaoh's heart? (3, 5)

3. How old was Moses and Aaron when they went before Pharaoh? (7)

4. What was the first miracle that God performed through Moses and how did the Egyptians contend with it? (9-12)

5. What was Moses commanded to do with his rod the second time? (17-21)

6. Was Pharaoh moved by this? (22)

7. How long was the water like this? (25)

Chapter 8 – The Plagues Of Frogs, Lice, And Flies

1. If Pharaoh refuses to let God's people go what fate will befall him? (1-4)

2. Why did the Lord cancel the frogs? (8-13)

3. Were the magicians able to duplicate this act? (7)

4. After Pharaoh's heart was hardened what was the next plague to descend upon the Egyptians? (16-17)

5. Were the magicians able to duplicate the plagues? (18)

6. What did the magicians conclude about the matter? (19)

7. What did the Lord command Moses to say at the water's edge? (20-21)

8. Why did the Lord not allow flies in the land of Goshen? (22)

Chapter 9 – Plagues On The Cattle, Boils, And Hail

1. What was the next tragedy to befall the Egyptians after Pharaoh's refusal to cooperate? (3)

2. What happened with the ashes of the furnace? (8-9)

3. Were the magicians equipped to handle this? (11)

4. What was the purpose of the plagues? (14)

5. Why was Pharaoh born? (16)

6. What was the next calamity in the land of Egypt? (18, 22, 23, 24)

7. Was anyone spared this fate? (19, 20, 26)

8. After the storm did Pharaoh let the people go? (35)

Chapter 10 – Plagues of Locusts and Darkness

1. Describe the next plague the Lord brought upon the land? (4,5,6)

2. What did Pharaoh's servants ask him to do? (7)

3. Who did Pharaoh give permission to leave with Moses and serve the Lord? (11)

Chapter 11 – Death of The Firstborn Threatened

1. How many more plagues was the Lord to bring upon Egypt? (1)

2. What were the Hebrews instructed to borrow (2) and why do you think the Egyptians were willing to comply? (3)

3. Explain what happened to the first born of the Egyptians and Hebrews? (5-7)

4. Did Pharaoh let the children of Israel go, why or why not? (10)

Chapter 12 – The Passover and Death of The Firstborn

1. What did the Lord do about the Egyptian calendar that the Hebrews were following? (2)

2. What instructions did the Lord give the Israelites regarding the lamb? (3-6)

3. What were they to do with the lamb's blood? (7)

4. How were they to eat this meal, and what was it called? (8-11)

5. What judgment was the Lord going to execute? (12)

6. How were the Hebrews protected? (13)

7. Describe what God commanded the Hebrews to do through the generations? (14-17)

8. The Holy Convocation was observed on what days? (16)

9. What is the fate of those who eat leavened bread? (19)

10. At what time did the Lord smite the first born of Egypt? (29)

11. When this started, who did Pharaoh call for? (31-32)

12. When and how did the Hebrews leave Egypt? (33-36)

13. How many people traveled from Ramses to Succoth and were the animals with them? (37-38)

14. How long were the Israelites in Egypt? (40)

15. What restrictions did the Lord put on the Passover? (42-51)

Chapter 13 – Pillar of Cloud and Pillar of Fire

1. What did the Lord require of the Hebrews? (1-2)

2. Summarize verses 3 through 18.

3. Whose bones were taken out of Egypt? (19)

4. Explain the function of the pillars of fire and clouds. (21-22)

Chapter 14 – The Red Sea

1. Where did the Lord tell the Hebrews to camp and for what purpose? (1-4)

2. After Pharaoh found out that the Hebrews fled Egypt what was his next course of action? (6-9)

3. What did the Hebrews speak out of fear to Moses? (11-12)

4. What did Moses answer? (13-14)

5. How were the children of Israel commanded to go forward and what miracle took place? (15-16)

6. Was there an angel of God assigned to the camp? (19)

7. How did the pillar of clouds appear to the Egyptians as compared to the Hebrews? (19-20)

8. How did the Lord part the sea? (21)

9. Describe the passage and pursuit. (22-23)

10. What did the Lord do to the chariots? (25)

11. What was the fate of the Egyptians? (26-27)

12. What conclusion did the children of Israel come to? (31)

Chapter 15 - Marah

1. What is being described in verses 1-19?

2. Where did the Israelites journey to and what was the condition of the place? (22)

3. What does Marah mean? (23)

4. What miracle was performed there? (25)

5. What did the Lord promise the Israelites? (26)

6. How did the Lord describe himself? (26)

7. What was found in Elam? (27)

Chapter 16 – The Wilderness Of Sin

1. When did the Israelites arrive in Sin? (1)

2. What type of attitude did they have? (2-3)

3. What was the Lord going to send from heaven and what was it purpose and what were the stipulations? (4-5)

4. What was to be seen in the morning? (7)

5. How did the Lord feed his people? (12-15)

6. What happened to the manna that was not eaten? (20-21)

7. How was the Sabbath observed? ((22-30)

8. What did manna look and taste like? (31)

9. How long did they eat it? (35)

Chapter 17 – Water and War

1. What were the children of Israel complaining about? (1-2)

2. How did Moses get water out of a rock? (6)

3. Who fought the Hebrews in Rephidim? (8)

4. How was the battle won? (9-13)

5. What did the Lord tell Moses to write and for what purpose? (14, 16)

6. What did Moses name the altar? (15)

Chapter 18 – Jethro and Judges

1. Who came to visit Moses in the new land? (1-5)

2. How did Jethro react to the news that Moses gave him? (9, 11)

3. What advice did Jethro give Moses about the way he judged the people? (17-23)

4. Did Moses take Jethro's advice and what was his role after this? (24, 26)

Chapter 19 – Mount Sinai

1. Where did Israel travel and camp in the third month? (1-2)

2. Who does the earth belong to? (5)

3. What did the Lord command Moses to tell his people? (4-6)

4. What was the purpose of the thick cloud? (9)

5. How were the people told to get ready for the visitation of the Lord? (10)

6. When and where was the Lord going to appear? (11)

7. What precautions were to be taken? (12-13)

8. What happened on the third day? (16-19)

9. What was Moses instructed to tell the people? (21, 22, 24)

Chapter 20 – The Law

1. How many gods are we allowed to worship? (3, 5)

2. What types of graven images are prohibited? (4)

3. For those who hate the Lord, how long will they be punished? (5)

4. Who does God show mercy to? (6)

5. How should we honor the Lord's name? (7)

6. How are we to observe the Sabbath? (8-10)

7. What did the Lord create in six days? (11)

8. How do we extend the years of our life in relationship to our parents? (12)

9. List the other commandments in verses 13 through 17.

10. What did the people see and what were they afraid of? (18-19)

11. How were the Israelites further instructed to worship God? (23-26)

Chapter 21- Laws

1. Read this chapter and determine if any of these laws are practiced today in the country/culture that you live in.

2. Verse 24 is often quoted in the American society to justify revenge. What are your thoughts?

Chapter 22 - Laws

1. Give your opinion about whether or not these laws should be practiced in the society in which you live.

Chapter 23 – An Angel Leads The People

1. Describe the significance of the number seven in verses 11, 12, and 15.

2. Describe the significance of the number three in verses 14 and 17.

3. What are we to do with the first fruits? (19)

4. What was the purpose of the angel and what were the Hebrews cautioned about? (20-23)

5. What did God promise the Hebrews if they kept his commandments? (25-26)

6. Why do you think the Lord told the Hebrews repeatedly not to worship other Gods? (13, 24, 33)

7. What is significant about the number of times they were warned?

Chapter 24 – Moses and Elders

1. Who worshiped with Moses? (1)

2. Describe how Moses prepared the people before he communed with God? (4-8)

3. Describe how God appeared to Moses, his ministers, and his elders? (10)

4. What did God tell Moses about the tables of stones? (12)

5. How long did the glory cloud cover Mt. Sinai? (16)

6. On what day did the Lord speak to Moses? (16)

7. How did the children of Israel see the glory? (17)

8. How long was Moses on the mount under the glory? (18)

Chapter 25 – The Sanctuary

1. The children of Israel were instructed to bring the Lord their best offering. What kind of offering do you bring to the Lord? (1-7)

2. The Israelites were given specific instructions about how to build the sanctuary and ark of the covenant. (8-21). Has the Lord given you specific instructions about your sanctuary or dwelling place?

3. Where was the Lord going to speak to the children when they worshiped Him? (22)

4. When was the show bread to be placed on the table? (30)

Chapter 26 – The Ark

1. Where was the ark of the testimony placed? (33)

2. What was the purpose of the veil? (33)

3. Where was the mercy seat and the ark of the testimony placed? (34)

Chapter 27 – The Alter

1. What instructions are given in this chapter of what is to be built? (1-19)

2. What kind of oil was to be used for the lamps? (20)

3. Who was assigned to make sure the light burned continually? (21)

Chapter 28 – The Priests' Garments

1. Who did the Lord call to be priests? (1)

2. How were they to be dressed? (4-8)

3. What was engraved on the two onyx stones? (9-10)

4. What was on the breastplate of judgment? (21)

5. Where and when was Aaron to wear the breastplate? (29)

6. What was Aaron's robe to be made of? (31)

7. Where were the bells to be placed and the purpose of the bells? (33-35)

8. How were Aaron's sons to be clothed? (40, 42)

9. How was Moses to treat the priests according to the Lord's directions? (41)

Chapter 29 - Consecration

1. This chapter describes the consecration of the priests. If you are a priest or minister, that is you hold the office of one of the five-fold ministry gifts, describe your consecration.

Chapter 30 – Incense, Offering, And Oil

1. Explain the rules of the altar of incense and where it was to be placed. (6-9)

2. Who was required to give and offering to the Lord? (14)

3. Was it based on their income? (15)

4. What was the purpose of the basin? (18-21)

5. Describe the ingredients of the anointing oil. (23-25)

6. What is to be anointed? (26-30)

7. What were the restrictions on the anointing oil? (32-33)

8. Describe the perfume, purpose, and restrictions that the Lord told Moses to make. (34-38)

Chapter 31- The Sabbath As A Sign

1. What did the Lord bestow upon Bezaleel and Aholiab? (1-11)

2. What did the Lord tell Moses about the Sabbath? (13-18)

Chapter 32 - Idolatry

1. The Israelites became uneasy when Moses did not return in a timely manner from Mount Sinai. What did Aaron make out of gold to appease the Israelites? (2-4)

2. How did the Israelites worship the image? (5-6)

3. What did the Lord tell Moses? (7-10)

4. Why did Moses ask the Lord to repent for his anger? (11-13)

5. How were the tablets of the testimony written? (15-16)

6. What happened to the tablets when Moses came down from the mount? (19-20)

7. What tribe decided to worship the Most High God? (26)

8. What happened to the others? (27-28)

9. What did the Lord do to the people because of their sin? (35)

Chapter 33- The Tabernacle

1. Where was Moses to lead the Israelites and who was to go before them? (1-3)

2. Why did the Israelites take off their jewelry? (4-6)

3. What did Moses ask of the Lord? (13, 18)

4. How did the Lord show himself to Moses? (20-23)

Chapter 34 – Instructions and Moses Before The Lord

1. What did the Lord instruct Moses to do? (1-3)

2. How did the Lord descend? (5)

3. How long are the sins of the fathers carried down the bloodline/generations? (7)

4. What did the Lord tell Moses he was going to do? (10)

5. What was the warning? (12-17)

6. What did the Lord command Moses to destroy? (13)

7. How long was Moses on the mount and why did he cover his face? (28-35)

Chapter 35 – The Sabbath

1. What were the regulations for the Sabbath? (2)

2. What were the instructions for the offering? (5-9)

3. How was the tabernacle to be arrayed? (10-19)

Chapter 36 – Offering and The Tabernacle

1. Why did Moses stop the offering for the sanctuary? (5, 7)

Summarize chapters 37-40. Be sure to include the priestly clothing, the tabernacle, consecration, and the glory cloud and its function.

THE TWELVE TRIBES OF ISRAEL

SONS		BIRTH MOTHER	
Name	**Meaning**	**Name**	**Meaning**
Reuben	behold a son	Leah	lothe, weary
Simeon	heard	Leah	
Levi	joined to	Leah	
Judah	praise	Leah	
Dan	a judge	Bilhah	to trouble, to terrify
Naphtali	wrestling	Bilhah	
Gad	troop	Zilpah	trickle, fragrant dropping
Asher	happy	Zilpah	
Issachar	no recompense	Leah	
Zebulun	exalted	Leah	
Joseph	Jehovah has added	Rachel	to journey, ewe
Benjamin	son of the right hand	Rachel	

(These are Jacob's sons listed in birth order).

When the names are translated, just as in every book of the Bible, the history of the person under study unfolds. The following is a brief account of Jacob's life which began in the book of Genesis.

Jacob received the blessing from his father Isaac because he was the son of his right hand. Jacob heard from the Lord in a dream which propelled him into his destiny. Jacob praised and exalted the Most High God and erected an altar in His name at Bethel. After Jacob's long journey he entered into the camp of Laban. There he fell in love with Rachel. Instead of trickling Laban with gifts in exchange for his daughter's hand in marriage, Jacob agreed to work for Laban for seven years. Jacob did not receive Rachel as his first wife as his recompense of reward. Jacob married Leah and they were happy to behold their first son, Reuben. During his troubled times Jacob joined with his wives Leah and Rachel and two of their hand maidens to birth a troop of 12 sons. When Jacob was in Peniel he wrestled with an angel until he became weary. Jehovah changed his name from Jacob to Israel, meaning prince. The Lord, Jehovah, did not judge him for his past deception with Esau but added the blessing of Abraham, the father of many nations. The legacy continued throughout the generations as Jacob became the prince of Israel.

THE TWELVE TRIBES OF ISHMAEL

Ishmael, Isaac's half-brother also had twelve sons which are listed below. The meaning of their names and a brief narrative of Ishmael's life when he lived with his mother, Hagar, is revealed in the names of Ishmael's sons.

Name	Meaning
Nebajoth	heights
Kadar	dark
Adbeel	chastened of God
Mibsam	sweet odor
Mishma	a hearing
Dumah	silence
Massa	burden
Hadar	honor
Tema	desert
Jehtur	enclosed
Naphish	refreshment
Kedemah	original (first)

Ishmael	God will hear
Hagar (his mother)	flight
Abram (his father)	exalted father
(Strong, 1990)	

When Hagar conceived Abram's son, Sarai became angry and Hagar took flight into the wilderness. Hagar was chastened by God, told to return to her mistress and bear the burden in silence. Hagar gave birth to Ishmael, Abram's first son. However, he did not receive the honor of his exalted father under the Abrahamic covenant.

Isaac was born fourteen years later and Sarah did not want Ishmael to have the same privileges as her son Isaac. Sarah reverted to her old ways and sent Ishmael and Hagar into the desert with very few provisions. During the darkest hour when their water was all gone, Hagar wept and enclosed Ishmael under a bush. At the height of her prayer, God heard her and gave them refreshment in a well of water. God explained Ishmael's destiny which was a sweet odor that permeated her dry parched soul.

THE FIRST TWELVE MIRACLES GOD PERFORMED THROUGH MOSES

	Miracle	Symbolism
1	Rod To Serpent	Rod - correction, rule
		Serpent – Satan
2	River To Blood	god of the river worshiped by Egyptians
3	Frogs	One of the Egyptian gods, unclean, witchcraft
4	Lice	demons, airborne pests, called finger of God by the magicians
5	Flies	Satan, airborne pests
6	The Cattle Die	Cattle were considered sacred
7	Boils	Spiritually unclean
8	Hail And Fire	Purification
9	Locusts	Destruction, famine
10	Three Days of Darkness	Hell - where there is no light (Jesus spends three days in hell after his death on the cross)
11	First Born of Man And Beast Dies	Death
12	The Red Sea Is Divided From East To West	Red symbolizes suffering and sacrifice
		The sea symbolizes wicked nations, East is associated with beginning, law, and birth

The number ten symbolizes law, the number twelve symbolizes government.
(Definitions were taken from: Price, 2006; The King James Study Bible, 1988)

There is a deeper meaning to the first twelve miracles than is listed above. In this account the Lord is trying to get the Egyptians to stop worshiping false gods and to follow Him. Read the word from the Lord.

The lord of the flies ruled over Egypt and deceived the people into worshiping false gods. The Egyptians saw cattle as sacred, and worshiped the god of the frogs, and the god of the river, and many other gods. These demonic forces ruled the land and the air. The Most High God sent correction through His servant Moses. His rod brought forth signs and wonders. Because of these false gods the people were spiritually unclean. The Lord rained down hail and fire to cleanse the land and to show his presence and majesty. The locusts brought famine, and the first born of man and beast died. As in the beginning, the first man Adam was deceived by the lord of the flies and went into spiritual darkness, from life to death. The finger of the Lord brought the law to rule and guide the people. In order to save the wicked nations, the Most High God, the Father of Lights sacrificed his only begotten son, who died, and spent three days in hell conquering the forces of darkness. The resurrection of Jesus Christ on the third day brought a new beginning and a new government that freed us from the lord of the flies.

THE TEN COMMANDMENTS
* Thou shall have no other gods before me
* Thou shall not make any graven images
* Thou shall not take the name of the Lord thy God in vain
* Thou shall not kill
* Thou shall not steal
* Honor thy father and thy mother that thy days be long upon the land which the Lord thy God giveth thee
* Thou shall not commit adultery
* Thou shall not bear false witness against thy neighbor
* Thou shall not covet thy neighbor's house, wife, or possesions
* Remember the Sabbath and keep it holy

GOD'S CALENDAR

After the flood, God changed the calendar to coincide with Noah's birth which occurred six hundred years prior. Because Noah and his family were the only people chosen to escape the flood and Noah was the oldest of his clan, it appeals to the human intellect that God would start numbering the years with his birth.

Before the exodus of the Hebrews, God removed them from the Egyptian calendar and put them back on His calendar. The following is a brief synopsis of what happened to Noah and his family and the Hebrews in the first two months of their lives when they began to live according to God's calendar.

Noah

- It began to rain on the seventeenth day of the second month in the six hundredth year of Noah's life (Genesis 7:11).
- Noah removed the covering of the ark on the first day of the first month, in the 601st year (Genesis 8:13).
- Noah and his family left the ark on the 27th day of the second month when the earth was dry(Genesis 8:14).

Moses and the Hebrews

- After the plague of darkness and before the death of the first-born, the Lord instructed Moses and Aaron about the calendar change. The Lord declared that the month was now the first month of the year, and that the Passover would begin on the fourteenth day of the first month (Exodus 12: 1-3) .
- The Feast of Unleavened Bread is to be observed on the 14th - 21st days of the first month of every year (Exodus 12:17-20).
- The Hebrews came out of bondage in the month of Abib, which is now called Nissan (Exodus 13:4). It was on the fifteenth day of the first month, on the morrow after the Passover (Numbers 33:3).
- The Hebrews are in the wilderness of Sin and the Lord feeds them with quail and manna, on the fifteenth day of the second month (Exodus 16).

The first month of the Hebrew calendar is called Nissan which is associated with months of March and April in the Gregorian calendar. The month of Nissan is also associated with the tribe of Judah which went first in battle. The Hebrew letter hei is associated with this month which means the window over you, with the wind of God blowing down on you.

The second month in the Hebrew calendar is Iyar which corresponds with the months of April and May in the Gregorian calendar. The month of Iyar is associated with the tribe of Issachar which knew the times and seasons. The Hebrew letter vav is associated with this month and it links redemption with giving.

When we look at the function of the tribes of Judah and Issachar along with the meaning of the letters of hei and vav, we are then able to see God's plan and purpose unfold. The aforementioned scriptures will be written again to include the information about the Hebrew tribes and the months.

Noah

- It began to rain on the seventeenth day of the second month in the six hundredth year of Noah's life (Genesis 7:11). *In the month of Iyar, the wind of God blew over them and brought the rain because it was the time and the season God had spoken of.*
- Noah removed the covering of the ark on the first day of the first month *of Nissan* in the 601ˢᵗ year (Genesis 8:13). *Noah removed the covering of the window of God.*
- Noah and his family left the ark on the 27ᵗʰ day of the second month when the earth was dry (Genesis 8:14). *It was time to begin God's redemptive plan. This was the first tribe who began to re-populate the earth after the flood in the month of Iyar, it was their time.*

Moses and the Hebrews

- After the plague of darkness and before the death of the firstborn, the Lord instructed Moses and Aaron about the calendar change. The Lord declared that the month was now the first month of the year, and that the Passover would begin on the fourteenth day of the first month. (Exodus 12:1-3, 17-20) The Feast of Unleavened Bread is to be observed on the 14th - 21st days of the first month of every year, *because this was God's time and God's calendar for His people in the month of Nissan.*
- The Hebrews came out of bondage in the month of Abib (Exodus 13:4). It was on the fifteenth day of the first month, on the morrow after the Passover (Numbers 33:3). *In the month of Nissan, God opened up a window and blew the east wind to part the Red Sea. These were the first descendants of the tribes of Israel to come out of bondage in over four hundred years.*
- When the Hebrews were in the wilderness of Sin and the Lord fed them with quail and manna, on the fifteenth day of the second month of Iyar (Exodus 16). *This began their season of wandering for forty years which was part of God's redemptive plan.*

HEBREW/JEWISH CALENDAR

MONTH	TRIBE	LETTER	GREGORIAN CALENDAR MONTH
Nissan or Abib	Judah	Hei	March/April
Iyar	Issachar	Vav	April/May
Sivan	Zebulun	Zayin	May/June
Tammuz	Reuben	Chet	June/July
Av	Simeon	Tet	July/August
Elul	Gad	Yud	August/September
Tishrel	Ephraim	Lamed	September/October
Cheshvan	Manasseh	Nun	October/November
Kislev	Benjamin	Samekh	November/December
Tevet	Dan	Ayin	December/January
Shevat	Asher	Tzadik	January/February
Adar	Naphtali	Kuf	February/March

HEBREW/JEWISH HOLY DAYS

The Hebrews started to be called Jews around 600 B.C. The name is taken from Judah, one of the twelve tribes of Israel. During the forty years of wandering in the desert, the tribe of Judah always went first in battle. Today, Judaism is the name used for the people and the religion who are the descendants of Abraham, Isaac, and Jacob. Judah is also the tribe which contains the genealogy of Jesus Christ. It is no mistake that God's chosen people retain the name from the Lion of the tribe of Judah as prophesied in Genesis 49: 8-10.

The Hebrew calendar is based on lunar months and the day begins at sundown as indicated in the book of Genesis. Therefore a Jewish holiday starts the night before the day listed on the calendar. Here is a brief description of some of the major Jewish holidays.

Sabbath or Shabbat

- A weekly seventh day of rest as written in Genesis 2:2-3, which is Saturday according to Jewish tradition.

Rosh Chodesh

- Head of the month as marked by the beginning of the new moon, which begins the first day of the lunar month. It is also called first fruits as it is a time to give the first fruit offering to the Lord

Pesach or Passover

- Is celebrated in March or April to commemorate the Jews coming out of bondage in Egypt. It begins on the 14th day of Nissan and is celebrated for eight days. The Sedar, the meal and the recounting of the Exodus, is observed on the eve of the Passover.

Shavuot or Pentecost

- Is celebrated in May or June which corresponds to the month of Sivan. It celebrates the giving of the Torah on Mt. Sinai and the outpouring of the Holy Spirit in Acts 2 for Christians. It is celebrated fifty days after Passover, or fifty days after Christ's Ascension for Christians.

Rosh Hashanah or the Head Of The Year

- Is celebrated on the first day of Tishrei in September.

Yom Kippur or the Day of Atonement

- It is celebrated on the 10th day of Tishrei in September or October with fasting and prayer for atonement of sins. The first ten days of the New Year are called the Days of Awe.

Chanukah

- It is an eight day festival that begins on the 25th day of Kislev or in December. It commemorates the rededication of the temple in Jerusalem that was taken back by the Maccabees.

(Definitions taken from Pierce, 2011; Webster, 1998).

SUMMARY QUESTIONS

1. There are many people of the world that live under very harsh conditions. Even though famine, natural disasters, and wars permeate their landscapes, their populations continue to explode. Identify at least three nations or countries where this is happening.

2. Were you ever sent away by your biological parents and for what purpose?

3. Is God calling you to reclaim your heritage?

4. Has God given you a mandate that you believe is too big for you to carry?

5. Do you have an "Aaron's rod" that will be a sign of God's omnipotent power?

6. Did you or someone you know ever complain to management about unfair labor practices?

7. If yes was there retaliation to you or your co-workers?

ROUTE OF THE EXODUS OF THE ISRAELITES FROM EGYPT

The grey arrows show the Exodus of the Israelites from Egypt to the Promised Land
(Taken from bible-history.com/maps/route_exodus)

CHAPTER SEVEN

THE BOOK OF REVELATION OF JESUS CHRIST

Step Seven: Rebuke The Devourer, The Lord Shall Reign Forever

The book of Revelation is about the judgment of God on the world, paganism, and the return of Christ. The following terms relate to the events in this book of scripture which are The Rapture, The Great Tribulation, and Armageddon. The first term is not mentioned but the events are described which were coined during the development of the church. Many theologians disagree on the timing of the events and who will and will not be raptured. Because these terms are used in sermons it is important to understand what is being preached.

The Rapture is defined as the church (Christians) being taken out of the earth, to be with Christ, this includes those who have died before the tribulation. The scripture most often quoted to describe this is I Thessalonians 4:17. This is also described as the numberless multitude in Revelation 7:9-17.

The Great Tribulation is a period of suffering sent by God to the people of the earth as described in Revelation chapters 6, 8, 9, and 11. Armageddon is the name for the final battle between God and the devil. It takes place after the thousand year reign of Christ as written in Revelation 16:14-16.

There are very few Pastors and teachers who will use this book as a subject matter for their Sunday sermons and Bible classes because of the complexity of the material. If you get discouraged and are not able to interpret the symbolism use a study Bible for this step. This step is one you can work for many years to come. As you grow in Christ your revelation of this book will become deeper.

This is the beginning of the second half of your twelve step program. This book will enlighten you like no other.

Chapter 1 – A Vision Of The Son Of Man

1. What is the purpose of the book of Revelation and what are the conditions of the prophecy? (1,3)

2. Which apostle wrote the book of Revelation? (2,4)

3. Who is Jesus and explain what He did for us? (5, 6)

4. How will Jesus return? (7)

5. How did John describe himself and where did he write this scripture? (9-10)

6. What instructions did John hear while he was in the spirit? (11, 19, 20)

7. What did John see when he turned around to see who was talking to him? (12-13)

8. Describe how John saw the Son of Man. (13-16)

9. What was the first thing the Lord said to John when he fell down at his feet? (17)

10. Who has the keys of hell and death? (18)

Chapter 2 – A Message To The Churches

1. What did Jesus explain to the head of the church at Ephesus? (2-3)

2. What was the church asked to repent for and what are the consequences if they do not? (4-5)

3. Who will be given the tree of life? (7)

4. How was the church in Smryna being prosecuted? (8-10)

5. For those who are faithful what shall be given to them? (10-11)

6. The next section is written to the church at Pergamos. Who is the person with the two edged sword? (12)

7. What is Jesus saying about the churches dichotomous nature? (13-14)

8. What will happen if this church fails to repent? (16)

9. What will be given to those that over come? (17)

10. What was wrong with the church at Thyatira? (19-20)

11. Was she given a chance to repent? (21)

12. What are the consequences for not obeying God? (22-23)

13. Who searches our hearts and rewards us according to our works? (23)

14. What was the fate of those who did not dance with the devil? (24)

15. Who will be given power over the nations, how will they rule and what will they be given? (26-28)

16. Which churches were into idol worship? (2:14, 2:20)

Chapter 3 – A Message To The Churches

1. What is the Lord saying to the Church at Sardis? (1-3)

2. For those who did not dishonor Jesus what will they be given? (4)

3. What will happen to the names of those who are worthy? (5)

4. What is Jesus saying to the church at Philadelphia? (7-8)

5. For those who kept God's commandments, how were they rewarded? (10)

6. What else is promised to those that overcometh? (12)

7. How will the city of God be formed and what is the name of the city? (12)

8. What is the Lord saying to the church at Laodicean? (15-16)

9. This church has not made a commitment whether to serve God or to serve the world. What do they talk about most? (17)

10. As you read verse eighteen, what do you think the Lord is trying to get the church to do?

11. If you repent and say yes to Jesus what is expected? (20-21)

Chapter 4 – God's Throne

1. John heard a voice as he looked up into heaven, describe. (1)

2. What did John see while he was in the spirit. (2)

3. What did the throne look like? (3)

4. How many elders were on the throne and how were they dressed? (4)

5. What came out of the throne? (6)

6. How many lamps were burning and what did they represent? (5)

7. What was in front of the throne? (6)

8. How many beasts were there and describe what they looked like and what they said? (7-8)

9. How did the elders respond to this? (10-11)

Chapter 5 – The Lion And The Lamb

1. What did the Father have in his right hand? (1)

2. What did the angel proclaim? (2)

3. Who was able to open the book? (3-4)

4. What did the elder proclaim in verse 5?

5. How did Jesus appear to John in the midst of the throne? (6)

6. What did the four beasts and elder do when Jesus took the book from the Father? (7-9)

7. Who were we made to be? (10)

8. How many beasts and angels were present and what did they say? (11-13)

Chapter 6 – The Beginning of Judgment of Unbelievers During The Tribulation.

1. What did John observe when the Lamb opened one of the seals? (1)

2. Describe the action of the white horse in verse 2.

3. After the second seal was opened what happened? (3-4)

4. Describe what happened after the third seal was opened. (5-6)

5. What color was the fourth horse and what was his purpose? (8)

6. What happened after the fifth seal was opened? (9-11)

7. What happened after the sixth seal was opened? (12-14)

8. How did the people of the earth react to this? (15-16)

9. What question was posed in verse seventeen?

Chapter 7 – The Tribes Of Israel And The Numberless Multitude

1. Describe what the four angels of the earth were doing? (1)

2. The angel ascended from the east. What type of seal did he have and what was his commission? (2-3)

3. Describe the tribes of Israel as given in verses four through eight.

4. How many other people came before the throne of God and what nations did they represent? (9)

5. How did the multitudes in heaven worship God? (10-12) Notice the seven-fold prayer.

6. Who was dressed in white robes and how did they get that way? (14)

7. What is their life like in heaven? (15-16)

8. What shall the Lamb do for them? (17)

Chapter 8 – Seven Angels

1. What happened after the seventh seal was opened? (1)

2. Seven angels were given seven trumpets, what was their mission? (3-5)

3. Describe the mission of the first four angels. (7-13)

Chapter 9 – The Great Tribulation

1. What happened after the fifth angel sounded? (1)

2. What happened after the bottomless pit was opened? (2-4)

3. What is the fate of those who do not have the seal of God on their foreheads? (5)

4. Is death an escape from the torment at this time? (6)

5. Describe what locusts look like. (7-10)

6. Who rules over the scorpions? (11)

7. What happened after the sixth angel blew his trumpet? (14-15)

8. How many soldiers were assigned to kill mankind? (16)

9. What did the rest of John's vision consist of? (17-19)

10. The people who were not killed by the plagues, did they repent and change their lifestyle? (20-21)

Chapter 10 – The Little Book

1. What did the angel do and how was he clothed as described in verses 1-3.

2. What happened after the seven sounds of thunder and what was John commanded to do? (4)

3. There was an angel positioned over the heaven and earth, what did he swear? (5-6)

4. What will be finished when the seventh angel sounds his trumpet? (6-7)

5. What did the voice from heaven tell John to do in verses 8-11.

Chapter 11- The Two Witnesses

1. How was John told to measure the temple? (1-2)

2. Who will be given power and how shall they prophesy? (3)

3. How are the two witnesses described? (3, 4, 6)

4. What happens if any man tries to hurt them? (5)

5. What happens after they finish their testimony? (8)

6. How are they buried? (8-10)

7. What happens after three days? (11-12)

8. When did the earthquake occur and how many were killed? (13)

9. How did the attitudes change of those who were not killed? (13b)

10. After the seventh angel blew his trumpet again what did the voices in heaven say? (15)

11. What did the twenty four elders do? (16-17)

12. Describe the time of judgment in verses 18 and 19.

Chapter 12 – The Woman And The Dragon

1. Describe the woman in the heavens. (1-2)

2. Describe the dragon in verse three.

3. Interpret verses 1 – 10 according to the following: the woman is Israel, the dragon is Lucifer, and the child is Jesus Christ.

4. How was he overcome? (11)

5. Why has the devil come down in great wrath and why did he persecute the woman that brought forth the man child? (12, 13)

6. Why did he make war on her seed? (15-17)

Chapter 13 – The Beasts

The first beast is the anti-Christ and the second beast is the false prophet.

1. What did John see come out of the sea? (1)

2. Where did the beast get his power? (2)

3. What happens to the beast in verse three and how is the entire world going to see this at the same time?

4. Why did the people worship the dragon? (4)

5. What was said about the Most High God and those that worship Him? (5-7)

6. Who will worship the Anti-Christ? (8)

7. What did the second beast look like? (11)

8. How did he influence the people? (12)

9. What powers did he possess? (13-15) The false prophet will fool the very elect.

10. What did the beast demand of the people? (16-17).

11. Many people believe that the "mark" is already in place and will be implanted later. What is your belief and what do you think it is?

• Satan perverts everything that God is and does. The trinity of the Most High God consists of God the Father, Jesus Christ the Son, and the Holy Spirit. The false trinity is: Satan (Father), the first beast is the Anti-Christ, and the second beast or false prophet, is the spirit.

Chapter 14 – The Voice of Many Waters

1. How many are redeemed from the earth and what did they sing? (1-5)

2. What was the job of the angel that was mentioned in verse six?

3. Why did Babylon fall? (8)

4. What will the Lord, the Lamb of God allow to happen to you if you accept the mark of the beast? (10-11)

5. What was John commanded to write in verse thirteen?

6. What did the angel say to the Son of Man and what happened next? (15-16)

7. Explain how the other angel appeared and what power he had? (18)

8. What happened after the sickle was thrust into the vines of the earth? (19-20)

Chapter 15 - Preparation

1. What were the seven angels holding? (1)

2. What did John observe over the sea of glass mingled with fire? (2)

3. What did the angels sing? (3-4)

4. What did John see in the tabernacle in heaven? (6-7)

5. What was the temple filled with and who was able to enter? (8)

Chapter 16 – The Battle of Armageddon

1. What did God command the angels to do? (1)

2. Explain what happened after the first three angels poured out the contents of their vials. (2-4)

3. What did the angels of the water declare? (5-6)

4. Explain what happened after angel four, five, and six poured out the contents of their vials. (8-12)

5. Describe what came out of the mouth of the dragon, the beast, and the false prophet. (13)

6. What are they showing the people? (14)

7. Where is the final battle of good and evil to be fought? (16)

8. What happened after the seventh angel poured out his vial? (17-18)

9. How was the great city divided and what happened to the other cities of the nations? (19)

10. What happened to Babylon, the islands, and mountains? (19-20)

11. How did the inhabitants of the earth respond to the hail storm? (21)

Chapter 17 - Babylon

1. What did the angel show John? (1-3)

2. Read verses 4-6. The interpretation is given in verses 7 -18.

Chapter 18 – Babylon Falls

1. What did the angel say in verses one and two?

2. What were all nations guilty of? (3)

3. What was another voice heard saying? (4-5)

4. What did Babylon say about herself? (7)

5. How will she be judged? (8)

6. When judgment comes how will the rulers and merchants of the earth react? (9-19)

7. Who did Babylon slay? (24)

8. What happened when a mighty angel threw a millstone into the sea? (21-23)

Chapter 19 – Marriage Supper Of The Lamb

1. What did John hear from the people in heaven? (1, 3)

2. How did the four beast and twenty four elders react? (4)

3. What did the voice say that came out of the throne room? (5-8)

4. What was John commanded to write? (9)

5. How is the spirit of prophecy defined? (10)

6. Describe the horse and the rider. (11-13)

7. Who is the word of God? (16)

8. What came out of his mouth and who followed him? (14-15)

9. What happened to the beast and false prophet those that worshiped them? (20-21)

Chapter 20 – Satan Bound

1. What did the angel do that had the key to the bottomless pit? (2- 3)

2. How long will he be bound and for what purpose? (2, 3, 7)

3. What kind of souls did John see? (4)

4. When does the first resurrection occur? (5)

5. Who shall reign with Christ? (6)

6. After Satan is set free what is to come? (8)

7. After Satan's brief rampage on earth what will happen to him? (10)

8. How were the dead judged? (12-13)

9. Who was cast into the lake of fire? (15)

Chapter 21 – A New Heaven and A New Earth

1. How did John see heaven, earth, and Jerusalem? (1-2)

2. What did the great voice say? (3-4)

3. What did he tell John to write? (5-7)

4. Who shall be in the lake of fire? (8)

5. Describe the holy city of Jerusalem. (10-11)

6. How was the city constructed? (12-21)

7. What did the temple look like? (22)

8. How long were the days and nights? (21:23, 21:25, 22:5)

9. Who is allowed into the city? (27)

Chapter 22 – Jesus Comes Quickly

1. What did the water look like? (1)

2. Describe the tree of life and the curse. (2-3)

3. Where will God's name be in the people that serve Him. (4)

4. What did the angel tell John after he fell down at his feet? (9)

5. What other instructions did John receive? (10)

6. What did Jesus say in the following verses? (12,13, 16, 20)

7. Who has a right to the tree of life? (14)

8. Who are the unbelievers? (15)

9. What did the spirit and the bride say? (17)

10. What will happen to those who add things to this prophecy? (18)

11. What will happen to those who omit things from this prophecy? (19)

Chart Summary

In the book of Revelation the number seven is significant because it symbolizes sovereignty, absoluteness, and divine revolutions and cycles. The following charts will help you retain and understand what you have studied in this book.

THE SEVEN CHURCHES

CHURCH	DESCRIPTION	INSTRUCTION	PROMISE
Ephesus	Rejected evil, had patience, and discernment	Repent and come back to Christ	The Tree Of Life
Smyrna	Blasphemous non-believers Suffering and poverty	Fear not, be faithful unto death	A Crown Of Life
Pergamos	They never denied Christ but are into idolatry, Fornication, and false doctrine. Satan's Seat	Repent	Hidden manna, white stone with a new name
Thyatira	Charity, patience, service and faith. Sacrificed unto Idols. Had Spirit of Jezebel	Hold fast, judgment comes on those who will not repent	Power over nations given Morning Star
Sardis	Works are known, but church is dead	Strengthen that which remains Holdfast and repent	White clothing, names confessed before God
Philadelphia	Kept God's word and did not deny Him Given name of God in New Jerusalem	God will make unbelievers Worship Him. Holdfast	Open door no man shuts Shut door no man opens
Laodicea	Lukewarm, focused on material wealth. Not aware of their limitations.	Repent and be zealous	Will share God's throne If they overcome

---

*The promises column is a description of Jesus Christ and his majesty

Dr. Julia Floyd Jones

Book of Revelation – The Seven Churches in the Province of Asia

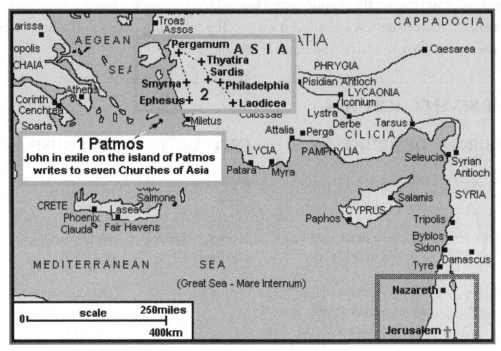

http://www.ccel.org/bible/phillips/JBPhillips.htm

THE SEVEN SEALS

Seals	The Effect On The Earth As The Seals Are Opened
First	Noise of thunder was heard as the seal was opened. He went forth conquering on a white horse.
Second	He was given a sword, and went out on a red horse and was given the power to take peace from the earth.
Third	He sat on a black horse with scales to measure wheat and barley. He was commanded to hurt not the oil and wine.
Fourth	Death sat on a pale horse and hell followed him. They were given power to kill ¼ of the earth.
Fifth	Under the altar the souls of those martyred for the Gospel cried out for justice. They were given white robes to rest for a little season.
Sixth	Great earthquakes, sun became black, moon became as blood, sky is rolled together like a scroll, and stars fell to earth. The mountains and islands are moved out of their place. All people become fearful.
Seventh	Silence in heaven for about thirty minutes. A golden censer filled with incense is offered with the prayers of the saints unto the altar of God. Then an angel takes the censer and fills it with fire and cast it upon the earth. There are voices (noises), thunder, lightning, and an earthquake.

*The seven seals are opened before the seven trumpets sound.

THE SEVEN TRUMPETS

Trumpets	The Effect Upon The Earth When The Trumpets Sound
First	Hail and fire mingled with blood, all green grass is burned and one third of trees are burned
Second	1/3 of sea became blood, 1/3 of sea life died, 1/3 of ships destroyed. During this time it sounded like a great mountain burning with fire that was cast into the sea.
Third	A burning star called Wormwood fell from heaven and fell on 1/3 part of rivers and fountains of waters. 1/3 of fresh water became bitter and many died.
Fourth	1/3 of sun destroyed, daylight shortened by 1/3, 1/3 of stars, 1/3 part of moon at night darkened
*Fifth	A star fell from heaven and was given a key to the bottomless pit. Locusts came out of the bottomless pit and were given power as the scorpions, and their king is Abaddon, also called Apollyon. They were commanded not to damage the grass, trees, or any green thing. They were able to torment non-Christians for five months. People will want to die but will not be able to.
*Sixth	Four angels in the Euphrates river were loosed to slay 1/3 part of men for one year, one month one day, and one hour. The army consists of 200,000,000 horsemen that kill by fire, smoke, and brimstone.
*Seventh	Voices in heaven said "the kingdoms of this world are become the kingdoms of our Lord, and of his Christ, and He shall reign forever and ever." The devil is released upon the earth with a great wrath and the anti-Christ begins his reign. He deceives many with miracles and institutes the mark of the beast in order for the people of the earth to buy or sell.

• Lucifer rebelled against the Most High God and was cast down from heaven with 1/3 of the angels which has an effect upon the earth even in the last days.

*These trumpets are either preceded or followed by "woe" which is defined as deep sorrow, grief, or calamity. Woe to the inhabitants of the earth is a warning of the increased torment and devastation to come. See Revelation 8:13, 11:14, and 12:12.

THE SEVEN LAST PLAGUES

VIAL	PLAGUE
First	Noisome and grievous sores came upon all those who had the mark of the beast and worshipped him.
Second	The vial was poured upon the sea and it became blood. Every living soul died in the sea.
Third	The vial was poured out upon the rivers and fountains and they became blood. The angels said this was a true and righteous judgment to avenge the saints and the prophets.
Fourth	The angel poured out his vial upon the sun to scorch people with fire and great heat. The people continued to curse the name of God and they did not repent.
Fifth	The vial was poured upon the seat of the beast and his kingdom was full of darkness. They blasphemed God because of their pain and sores and repented not.
Sixth	The vial was poured upon the River Euphrates and dried it up. *Unclean spirits came out of the mouth of the dragon, the beast and the false prophet. The spirits of devils performed miracles throughout the world and gathered the armies for the battle of Armageddon.
Seventh	The vial was poured into the air. A great voice from the throne room of heaven said "It is done." There were great noises, thunder, lightning, earthquakes that have never been seen before. Babylon was divided into three parts and the islands and mountains were not found. Hail stones came down from heaven that were 60 to 100 pounds (a talent). People continued to blaspheme God because of the hail.

*Satan perverts everything that God is and does. The trinity of the Most High God consists of God the Father, Jesus Christ the Son, and the Holy Spirit. The false trinity is: Satan (Father), the first beast is the Anti-Christ, and the second beast or false prophet, is the spirit.

Compare these to the Plagues of Egypt in Exodus 6-14.

Congratulations! You have completed one of the most difficult books in the Bible. You may have only peeled back one layer but that is fine. You have given yourself a good foundation for future study.

If nothing else is apparent to you, please understand that we are in a spiritual war. You have been commissioned into the army of the Lord Jesus Christ. It is your assignment to help win souls for the end time harvest. Do not march out in fear, but with confidence and boldness of who you are in Jesus.

The attacks will be many but don't give up the fight. Remember that the battle is already won. The enemy has been defeated **and the Lord will reign forever!** Rejoice for the glory of the Lord is upon you!

$\mathcal{T}$HE GOSPEL ACCORDING TO MATTHEW

Step Eight: Submit To God And To Him Alone

The book of Matthew begins with the genealogy of Jesus Christ. There are fourteen generations from Abraham to David, then fourteen generations from David to exile in Babylon and fourteen more generations from the exile to Christ. Notice there are three sets of fourteen representing God and humanity as tri-part beings. Four represents world-wide impact and ten represents God's Divine Law, hence the significance of the number fourteen. Jesus, the Son of God has impacted the four corners of the world. He brought healing, deliverance, salvation, and the working of miracles. He instructed us how to pray, treat each other, and live according to the Kingdom of Heaven which is God's divine law.

In this section for the book of Matthew, summaries and charts will be included after each chapter for clarity and to facilitate revelation knowledge.

Chapter 1 - Joseph

As discussed earlier, birth order is important. The twins Pharez and Zerah were born of Judah and Pharez was born first. Zerah's lineage is not written about in the genealogy of Jesus. (3-4)

1. Who were Jesus' earthly parents and how was he conceived? (18)

2. What did the angel of the Lord tell Joseph? (20-23)

3. What does Emanuel mean? (23)

4. What was Jesus' purpose? (21)

Chapter 2 – Jesus' Birth And The Wise men

1. Where was Jesus born, where did the wise men come from, and who was king at the time? (1)

2. Where did the wise men see the star? (2) (Note: the scripture does not say "three" wise men)

3. What did the wise men call Jesus and why do you think Herod was troubled by this? (2)

4. What type of gifts did the men from the east give Jesus? (11)

5. Why did the wise men not return to Herod? (12)

6. Why did Joseph take his family to Egypt? (13)

7. How did Herod respond when he found out that the men from the east did not return to him? (16)

8. After Herod died, what did the angel tell Joseph to do? (19-20)

9. Where did Joseph take his family to live? (22-23)

Chapter 3 – John The Baptist

1. Where and what did John the Baptist Preach? (1-3)

2. What did he wear and what did his diet consist of? (4)

3. Where were the people from that John baptized in the Jordan river? (5)

4. What did he call the Pharisees and Sadducees when they came to be baptized? (7)

5. What did he tell them to do before baptism? (8)

6. Who was John talking about in verse 11?

7. Jesus came from Galilee to be baptized by John in the Jordan. Did John feel worthy and how did Jesus respond? (14-15)

8. What happened in the heavenlies after Jesus' baptism? (16-17)

Chapter 4 – Jesus Begins His Ministry

1. How long did Jesus fast when he went into the wilderness? (2)
   (*The number forty represents purification, a period of spiritual preparation*)

2. Who is the tempter? (3)

3. Read verse four in this chapter. Then read Deuteronomy 8:3. Meditate on these scriptures. What is God speaking to you now?

4. List the ways Satan tempted Jesus in verses 3, 6, and 9.

5. List Jesus' answers in verses 4, 7, and 10.

The Lord wants the significance of the number of the bible verses explained in this section so that you may understand that the Holy Bible is truly the Word of God and that many Bible Codes exist that have not yet been revealed.

THE TEMPTATIONS AND THE SIGNIFICANCE OF THE NUMBERED VERSES

- Three - the trinity, the number of the God-head, indivisible power
- Four - worldwide impact

  In Matthew **4:3**, Satan ask Jesus, *"if thou be the son of God"* questioning if He is part of the God-head. Jesus is the second member of the eternal God-head. First there is God the Father, Jesus the Son is second, and the Holy Spirit is the third member of the eternal God-head. Together they are one, with indivisible power. The gospel of Jesus Christ has the power to change the world.

- Six - the number of flesh and humanity
  In Matthew **4:6**, Satan ask Jesus again, "*if thou be the Son of God*". Jesus was all God and all man, a member of humanity. He is also called the Son of Man. There is no doubt that Jesus came to save the world from Satan. He is the Son of God.

- Nine - the number of gestation, birthing, reproduction, and natural development
  In Matthew **4:9**, Satan promised Jesus all the kingdoms of the world if he would bow down and worship him. Jesus was born into this world to take back what Adam lost. Jesus is God and therefore all things in heaven and earth belong to Him, and all kingdoms of the world. Through his death, burial and resurrection all power is given to us who believe, to those who have been born again. It is a covenant promise that you will inherit the kingdom of heaven once you ask Jesus to come into your heart.

JESUS' ANSWERS TO THE TEMPTATIONS AND THE SIGNIFICANCE OF THE NUMBERED VERSES

- Four - represents worldwide impact, four corners of the world: north, south, east, west
  In Matthew **4:4**, Jesus said, "*man shall not live by bread alone, but by every word that proceedeth out of the mouth of God.*" The Word of God is quick and powerful and sharper than a two-edged sword and can effect change in the four corners of the earth, under the earth, and in the heavenlies. Our spirit must be fed as well as our physical body. Our spirit is to be fed by the Word of God which is the bread of life.

- Seven - The number of sovereignty and absoluteness
  In Matthew **4:7**, Jesus said, "*thou shall not tempt the Lord thy God.*" Jesus is absolutely the Son of God and He is sovereign and He reigns!

- Ten - God's Divine law
  In Matthew **4:10**, Jesus said "*thou shalt worship the Lord thy God and him only shalt thou serve.*" This is written in The 10 Commandments as; Thou shall have no other gods before Me. Who do you worship?

6. After the devil left Jesus, who came to minister unto Him, and why do you think that was important? (11)

7. After John the Baptist was thrown in prison, what did Jesus begin to preach, and why? (17)

8. In this chapter Jesus recruited four disciples, name them. (18, 21)

9. What did James preach in the synagogues of Galilee (23) and who was healed? (23-24)

In this chapter it is quite evident that the devil can quote scripture. When you are confronted by the enemy what will you do? Also notice that Jesus quoted scripture without using chapter and verse. He simply said "It is written." Add that to your arsenal.

Chapter 5

This chapter is often referred to as the Sermon on the Mount. **These scriptures are the answers to life's questions.** The following versions of the Bible will work the best for this chapter: NKJV, KJV, NIV. The questions are written for you. The answer to the question is located in the same verse unless otherwise indicated. Read the B portion of each verse as a question and then the A portion as the answer. Verses three through eleven are commonly referred to as The Beatitudes which means blessings.

1. Who has the kingdom of heaven? (3)

2. Who shall be comforted? (4)

3. Who shall inherit the earth? (5)

4. Who shall be filled? (6)

5. Who shall obtain mercy? (7)

6. Who shall see God? (8)

7. Who shall be called the children of God? (9)

8. Who does the kingdom of heaven belong to? (10)

9. What shall happen to you for Jesus' sake? (11)

10. How should we respond to the persecution of the prophets who came before us? (12)

11. Why should the salt of the earth be trodden under the foot of men? (13)

12. Who is the salt of the earth? (13)

13. Who is the light of the world? (14)

14. Can a city on a hill be hid? (14)

15. What gives light to all that are in the house? (15)

16. How do you glorify your Father which is in heaven? (16)

17. What did Jesus come not to destroy? (17)

18. What will not pass till all is fulfilled? (18)

19. Who is least and great in the kingdom of heaven? (19)

20. How does one enter into the kingdom of heaven? (20)

21. Who is in danger of the judgment and what is the commandment? (21)

22. Who shall be in danger of the judgment, council, and hell fire? (22)

23. What should you do if your brother has something against you? (23a, 24)

24. Why agree with the adversary quickly? (25)

25. What is the commandment in this verse? (27)

26. How do you commit adultery in your heart? (28)

27. How do you keep your whole body from perishing? (29)

28. Under what circumstances are you allowed to give your spouse a divorce? (31)

29. List the reasons and ways not to swear. (34-36)

30. What does an eye for an eye, and a tooth for a tooth mean? (38)

31. How did Jesus tell us to handle this? (39)

32. How should we respond when we believe others are asking too much of us? (40-42)

33. How are we instructed to treat our enemies? (43-44)

34. Does God discriminate between the just and unjust and what are we to do? (45, 48)

Chapter 6 - In this chapter Jesus instructs us how to pray, fast, and live by faith.

1. Read verses 1 - 8. What is the Lord speaking to you now?

2. What is known as The Lord's prayer is written in verses 9 - 13. If you do not know this prayer, commit it to memory and keep it in your heart.

3. What is the importance of forgiveness? (14-15)

4. How should one fast? (16-18)

5. Where should your treasure be? (19-21)

6. The eyes are the window to the soul. What is reflected in your eyes? (22-23)

7. What are the consequences of having one foot in the kingdom and one foot in the world? (24)

8. Is worry effective? (27)

9. Verses 24 - 34 tell you how to live by faith. How has God promised to take care of you? (25, 26, 28, 30)

10. Are you in need of food, clothing, or shelter?

- **Stand on the Word of God and remind Him of his Word and He shall perform it. By faith, believe that you receive it.**
- **Write down your request and then re-read verses 31-33. This is your answer. Wait for the manifestation of God's glory.**

Chapter 7 – Divine Cycles

1. Are you over-focused on what others are doing, if so how? (3-5)

2. Are you pointing the finger and being judgmental, if so how? (1-2)

3. The number seven symbolizes Divine revolutions and cycles as well as absoluteness. In Matthew 7:7 the Lord has stated that this verse is **absolutely so** because it completes a Divine cycle, His Divine cycle.

Action	Reaction
Ask	Given
Seek	Find
Knock	Opened

   Make your request known to God by following the above example. Notice that **ask (A, S, and K)** is also an acronym for **ask, seek, and knock**.

   The following scriptures state that there are many sins that lead to destruction (13). Few people are able to live a holy and righteous life. (14)

4. Who will come to you in sheep's clothing? (15)

5. How will you know them? (16-17)

6. How does one enter into the kingdom of heaven? (21)

7. What foundation is needed to weather the storms of life? (25)

8. In what manner did Jesus teach and how was he received? (28-29)

Chapter 8 - Healing

1. Is the Lord willing to heal you? (3, 7, 13, 15)

2. Who was healed in this chapter? (2, 5, 14, 16)

3. What was the leper instructed to do after he received his healing? (4)

4. Does Jesus need to be physically present to heal you? (8)

> You have authority over the devil. The Lord has given you dominion as a born again believer in Jesus Christ. There is power in the spoken word and the centurion understood this concept. When you have authority others will listen and obey. Declare your healing now. Command your body to line up with the Word of the Living God. God has already spoken it. Receive it now by faith.

5. Jesus' healing ministry was first spoken by the prophet Isaiah. (See Isaiah 53:4) If you have already decided to follow Jesus then when will you rest? Meditate on verse 20 for the answer.

6. What does verse 22 mean to you?

7. During the "storms of life" are you able to sleep? (24)

8. During times like this it is common for fear to creep in. When that happens who do you call? (25)

9. Even demons know that Jesus is the Son of God. Who among you doubts that He is the Son of God? (29)

10. The two men that were demon possessed were delivered by one word "go." (32)

    What is the one word that you need to hear from God in order to be set free?

11. If you decide to live like swine then what is your fate? (32)

12. What people do you know of today that if they were to become a born again believer would influence multitudes to follow Jesus? (33, 34)

Chapter 9 – Signs and Wonders
1. Can God read your thoughts? (4)

    Therefore nothing is really done in secret.

2. Have you repented for your sins and asked God to forgive you? (2, 5, 6)

If so then rise up and walk!

3. When you were born again you became a new creature in Christ. He has cleansed you of your past and poured his Spirit into a clean vessel. (15-17)

Then, be made whole.

4. Why did Jesus minister to the publicans and sinners? (12)

5. Are you operating in your ministry gifts and who are you ministering to?

6. What did the religious people accuse Jesus of? (34)

7. What did Jesus continue to do? (35)

8. Are there enough fisher of men to preach and heal the sick? (37-38)

Let us look at how healing took place in this chapter.

Sickness	Method of Healing
(2) A man sick with palsy	Forgiveness of sins
(18) A ruler's dead daughter	Laying on of hands
(20) Woman with an issue of blood	Faith and touching hem of garment
	(Same as a prayer cloth or a point of contact)

| (28) Two blind men | Faith and laying on of hands |
| (32) Dumb (mute) man | Casting out demons |

Healing took place by the Word, the Blood, and the Lamb. The Word of God (Jesus) became flesh and dwelt among us. Jesus is the Lamb of God. Jesus shed his blood for us and died on the cross, as a sacrificial offering, so that we could be healed, delivered, and set free. The blood of the Lamb healed the woman with an issue of blood. The spoken Word was able to cast out the demons and the man was able to speak after his deliverance (exorcism). This is a double entendre because Jesus is the Word of God! The words Jesus spoke forced the demons to come out of that man. Jesus is the name above every name. Jesus is the Word, the Blood, and the Lamb.

As previously shown there is more than one way to usher in healing. What method have you chosen? Some of you believe that you will not be healed until the person with the international healing ministry comes to a city near you, while others are waiting for the prayer cloth to come in the mail. Many people will be making a pilgrimage to a city to climb a mountain in their bare feet in an act of humility, believing the healing will take place once you reach the top of the mountain with the cross. The Lord is saying to go beyond the cross in your prayer time. The Lord says to ask, seek, knock, and receive.

Chapter 10 – The Twelve Disciples
1. List the twelve disciples. (2-4)

2. What did Jesus anoint them to do? (1)

3. Jesus gave the disciples several directives what were they? (5) These are for you as well.

4. Who were they to preach to? (6)

5. What subject were they to preach? (7)

6. Who were they to heal? (8)

7. What were they to do about provisions? (9-10)

8. Where should they stay? (11)

9. What should their attitudes be if they are not received well? (14)

10. What mind-set were they to adopt? (16)

11. What is expecting after preaching the word of God? (17-18)

12. When they are asked to defend themselves what should be said? (20)

13. Who will come against them? (21-23)

14. Why should you not fear people? (26)

15. Who is able to destroy the soul and the body? (28)

16. What is to be preached upon the housetops? (27)

17. What are the benefits of confessing that Jesus is the Son of God? (32-33)

18. What is the sword of the Lord? (34)

19. Where will your greatest foes be found and why is this so? (36)

    If you have accepted your calling and live by the word of God then whoever receives you receives Christ. Whoever receives Christ receives the most High God. (39-40)

Chapter 11 – John The Baptist

1. John the Baptist sent two of his disciples to ask Jesus if he was the one. Why do you believe that he doubted at this moment? (2-3)

2. How did Jesus' answer convey that John had first- hand experience of who Jesus was? (4)

3. Who prepared the way for Jesus as He spoke to the multitudes? (10)

4. Who was the last prophet to speak about Jesus before the prophecy was fulfilled? (13)

5. Why wasn't John received as a prophet? (18)

6. Why wasn't Jesus received as the Son of Man? (19)

7. Who does Jesus receive his gifts from? (27)

8. How do we access God the Father? (27)

9. What are we to do with our heavy burdens? (28-30)

Chapter 12 – Jesus Heals And Teaches

1. Why did the Pharisees scold the disciples? (1-2)

2. Why did Jesus quote scripture about what was done on the Sabbath? (4-7)

3. The Pharisees were religious and legalistic people, keeping tradition for tradition's sake. Did their attitudes and belief system prevent them from seeing that Jesus was the son of God? (8)

4. According to the Pharisees how did Jesus and his disciples not keep the Sabbath? (1, 10, 13)

5. How did the deaf and dumb man receive his healing? (22)

6. Who did the Pharisees credit with this power? (24)

7. Explain how Jesus rebuked them? (25- 30)

8. What sin is not forgiven? (31-32)

9. Are we held accountable for what we say? (36)

10. Jesus spoke a self-fulfilling prophecy, what was it? (40)

11. Jesus' mother and brother did not ask for special attention when they saw him on the street preaching. Why do you believe they behaved this way? (46-50)

In verses 43-45 Jesus speaks about the process of deliverance, also known as exorcism. Once you have been delivered from your strongholds do not go back. If you return to sin once your soul has been delivered from the power of darkness the demons will return to you seven-fold.

For those of you with any type of addiction you know this to be true especially if you have had a lengthy sobriety before relapse. Once you start using again you will start using at the same level of intensity as your last use. Deliverance is not to be taken lightly. It is important that you respect the process and the word of God.

Chapter 13 - Parables

1. Why did Jesus speak in parables? (11, 12, 13)

2. How do you receive things you don't want to hear?

3. What does this parable mean to you: the kingdom of heaven is like a grain of mustard seed? (31-32)

4. What does this parable mean to you: the kingdom of heaven is like unto leaven? (33)

5. What is God speaking to you in the parable of the sower? (37-42)

6. Describe what the kingdom of heaven is like? (41-42, 49-50)

7. Have you done mighty works for the kingdom in the secular world? How have the people you grew up with received you?

8. Why wasn't Jesus able to heal and perform miracles with this crowd? (58)

9. Were you ever hindered in your work by the home crowd?

Chapter 14 – Feeding The Multitudes

1. Who did Herod the Tetrarch believe Jesus to be? (1-2)

2. Why did Herod put John the Baptist in prison? (3-4)

3. The daughter of Herodias danced for King Herod on his birthday. What did he promise and what did she ask? (6-8)

4. How was the promise carried out? (10-11)

5. What did Jesus do when he heard of this? (13)

6. Why was Jesus moved with compassion? (14)

7. How did Jesus feed the multitudes? (17-19)

8. How many baskets were left over and how many disciples were there? How many people were gathered there? (20, 21)

9. What did Jesus do after he sent the multitudes away? (23)

10. Where were the disciples? (22)

11. What time did Jesus go to the ship and by what manner? (25)

12. What happened to Peter? (28-31)

13. How did this experience affect the other disciples? (33)

14. What happened in the land of Gennesaret? (34-36)

Twelve symbolizes divine government, five represents grace, and two represents covenant. Because believers have a covenant with God, He has given us grace and will take care of all our needs as long as we follow His divine government, laws, and commandments.

Chapter 15 – The Canaanite Woman

1. What did the Pharisees accuse the disciples of? (2)

2. How did the Pharisees' tradition effect the commandments? (6)

3. What was prophesied about the people from the prophet Isaiah (Esaias is Greek for Isaiah) (8-9)

4. What defiles a man? (11)

5. When you track the doctrines of men (9) what happens? (13-14)

6. What did the woman of Canaan want? (22)

7. How did Jesus respond to her? (23, 26)

8. Why was the Canaanite woman's daughter made whole? (28)

9. How did Jesus feed the crowd of people that followed him? (32-37)

10. How many baskets were left over this time and why is that significant? (32)

11. What made the people glorify God? (31)

12. How many people were fed? (38)

Seven loaves of bread and two fish were used to feed the people at this meeting. There were seven disciples present and seven baskets were left over at the end. If you recall earlier in the chapter the number seven represents Divine Sovereignty and a Divine Cycle which is completion. A fish is symbolic for Christianity and human souls under the lordship of Jesus Christ.

The seven disciples who were fisher of men used the word of God as a net to gather souls into the kingdom of God. The multitudes received food for their spirit, soul, and body. Fish from the sea were used to feed the physical body. Even today, fisher of men feed the soul and the spirit under the Lordship of Jesus Christ. Seven baskets were left over so that each disciple had his own provisions. The Lord will take care of you and multiply what you give to others if you just ask, pray, believe, and give thanks.

Chapter 16 – Pharisees and Sadducees

1. Jesus spoke with another group of Sadducees and Pharisees on the coast of Magdala. What happened with this group of people? (1-4)

2. Jesus warned the disciples to beware of the leaven of the Pharisees, what did He mean? (6,12)

3. How did the disciples answer when Jesus asked them who the people thought he was? (14)

4. Who revealed to Peter that Christ is the Son of the living God? (16-17)

5. What does Peter's name mean?

6. What should we expect when we are given the kingdom of heaven? (19)

7. What did Jesus prophesy to his disciples about what is to come? (21)

8. Peter took Jesus aside and rebuked him. What did Jesus say to Peter at this moment? (23)

9. Who are you following, God or the world?

10. If Jesus were to return today, would you be ready?

Chapter 17 - Transfiguration

1. After six days what disciples did Jesus take to the mountains? (1)

2. Describe what happened next. (2-7)

3. When Jesus comes back again do you think that the world will know him? (11-12)

4. What was the boy cured of and how? (15, 18)

5. Why were the disciples unable to cast them out? (20-21)

6. Jesus prophesied about things to come. Why do you think he mentioned it again? (22-23)

7. Do you pay your taxes? Do you pay your tithes? (24-27)

If yes to the first question and no to the second, explain your reasoning.

There are several layers of meanings to verses 1-12.

Six days, three disciples, and three people on the mountain
Meaning of the Names
Moses - a deliverer and a prophet
Elias (Elijah) - an Old Testament prophet that preached repentance and performed miracles. He also urged the people to return to the one true, living God.
John - God is gracious
Jesus - Deliverer, savior, the last Adam, the last sacrifice
Peter - the rock
James - supplanter, to take the place of, supercede
White - purity, triumph, victory
Transfiguration - change into another form

When Jesus stood on the Mount of Transfiguration with Moses and Elijah, his physical body was transformed as the glory of God enveloped his body. Jesus had the characteristics of Moses and Elijah and more. Jesus preached repentance and performed many miracles like Elijah before Him. Moses delivered God's chosen people out of bondage. Jesus, our deliverer, and our savior was pure and knew no sin. He took our place and became sin as the last and final sacrifice to save humanity from spiritual bondage. Jesus has triumphed over the enemy so that we can return to the one true living God. Because of His grace, we Christians have eternal life. He is the rock of our salvation and in Him we triumph and have victory.

There were two other people on the Mt. of Transfiguration. This was a precursor to what happened at the cross. Then there were two other people on the hill of Golgotha when Jesus was crucified. He was transfigured from life to death and back to eternal life (This will be discussed in chapter 27).

Chapter 18 – Temptation And Forgiveness

1. Who did Jesus say is greatest in the kingdom of heaven? (3-5)

2. What do verses 8 and 9 mean to you?

3. For those of you who have been called to the ministry and have not heeded the call are you lost? Can you hear your Shepard calling you? (11-14)

4. Are you still living a sinful life? In order to remove yourself from a life of sin it may be necessary not to associate with family and friends who will not lead a Godly life. If you choose not to do this, then you are likely to continue in the negative behavior. Ungodly behavior practiced long enough becomes comfortable and normal for those in the midst of it. (7-9)

5. What needs to be done in order for your prayers to be answered? (19-20)

6. How many times should you forgive those who offend you? (22)

70 X 7 = 490
Seven - Divine Cycles, absoluteness
Ten - God's Divine law
Four - a Divine command

Nine - gestation, reproduction, mature development

Jesus has given us a divine command to forgive the person who has offended us until we or the other person have matured or completed a Divine cycle by producing something new, i.e. a new behavior or attitude.

Forgiveness is a Divine Law. It has power in the spiritual realm to break strongholds. When you are full of unforgiveness and bitterness you will allow sickness and disease to develop in your body. What sickness are you suffering from? Is it curable and how?

7. What happens in the heavenly realm if you do not forgive? (34-35)

Chapter 19 – Divorce, Children, And The Rich Young Ruler

1. As usual the Pharisees came up with a question trying to get Jesus to contradict the scriptures. What is the only reason divorce is permitted? (9)

2. Who did Jesus heal in Judae and Jordan? (2, 13,)

3. Jesus quoted five of the Ten Commandments and a commandment that was first written in Leviticus 19:18, to the rich man. (18-19)

4. Why do you think Jesus quoted only the commandments the rich man was keeping?

5. Which commandment was the rich man guilty of breaking?

This is the answer to why he could not sell all that he had and follow Jesus.

6. Which commandments are you keeping and what are you going to do about the rest?

7. Are you willing to sell all of your possessions and follow Jesus?

8. Write down the names of three to five wealthy people. Who or what do they most trust, the stock market, real estate, higher education, etc., or God? (23-24).

   Do they acknowledge God privately or publicly for their success in life?

9. What was promised to the twelve disciples in heaven? (28)

10. What will the rest of us receive? (29)

Chapter 20 – Preaching And Healing

1. The kingdom of heaven does not reward us according to the world's system, explain. (1-16)

2. What did Jesus prepare the disciples for again and why? (18-19)

3. Who decides our place in heaven? (23)

4. What did Jesus feel in his heart before he healed? (34)

Chapter 21- The Authority Of Jesus

1. How did Jesus arrive into the city of Jerusalem? (2-8)

2. Hosanna is Hebrew for, save now, and deliver now. Explain what the multitudes were saying as Jesus entered into Jerusalem.

3. What happened in the temple? (12-15)

4. What are Christians able to do if there is faith without doubt? (21-22)

5. For those of you who operate in the gifts of the spirit, do the religious folks ever ask you by what authority you operate in your gifts? (24-27)

6. Jesus was very stern with the chief priests and elders. Why did he tell them that the publicans and harlots would enter the kingdom of God before them? (28-32)

7. Read verses 42-44. Write down what the parable means to you.

> **Author's Interpretation**
>
> The Kingdom of Heaven was first preached by the Jews but they rejected God's Son and orchestrated his death. The Kingdom of God was then preached by a new people, Christian people, followers of Jesus.
>
> Jesus is our cornerstone, the rock of our salvation. Whosoever shall fall on this stone shall be broken, that is our ungodly ways will be broken off of us so that Jesus can make us brand new. If it is necessary for Jesus to stop your evil ways, He will grind you to a halt and render you powerless.

8. Why did the chief priests and Pharisees decide not to harm Jesus? (46)

Chapter 22 – Parable and The Great Commandment
Read verses 2- 14.

1. What is your interpretation of the parable?

> **Author's Interpretation**
>
> The Kingdom of heaven was prepared for the people of the earth. God sent many prophets to invite the people into the kingdom but many of them would not come. Many of his prophets were slain because the people did not take the invitation into the kingdom seriously. God became angry and destroyed the people (just like in Sodom and Gomorrah). Other servants of God were sent out to preach the Word and many people decided to enter into the kingdom by making covenant with the King of Kings.
>
> There are wolves in sheep's clothing who will come into the church or your lives who will not confess that Jesus is the son of God. Bind that demonic spirit and cast it back to whence it came. Many people are invited into the Kingdom of God but few will accept the invitation.

2. Read verses 15-21 what do they mean to you?

3. Who are we married to in heaven? (22-31)

4. Who is the God of the living? (32)

5. What is the greatest commandment? (38)

6. What is the second? (39)

7. When Jesus asked the Pharisees who Christ's father is how did they answer and what did Jesus say after that? (42-46)

Chapter 23 – Denunciation Of The Scribes And Pharisees
Read verses 1- 14.

1. The Scribes and Pharisees do what needs to be done in order to be seen and look good for other people. What were they guilty of? (13-14)

2. If you swear by heaven, what else are you swearing by? (22)

3. What did the Pharisees omit? (23)

4. What do verses 24 - 38 mean to you?

5. Who is blessed? (39)

Chapter 24 – Destruction Of The Temple

1. What signs will usher in the end of the world? (5 - 7, 24)

2. At that time, what type of negative attitudes will we see among the people of the world? (9 - 12)

3. What happens to those that endure until the end? (13)

4. How is the gospel to be preached? (14)

5. Which prophet did Jesus say spoke of the end of time? (15)

The tribulation is described in verses 21, 22, 29, 40, and 41.

6. Who knows when Jesus will return? (36, 42, 44)

7. How will the Son of Man arrive after the great tribulation? (27, 29 - 33)

8. When will this generation pass and how will the Word of God pass away? (34-35)

Compare this section to Revelation 6:2-6; 7:11, 13; 8:2; 11:15, and 13:13.

Chapter 25

1. Read verses 1 - 13. Write down your interpretation before reading the author's interpretation.

Author's Interpretation

There were ten church folk also known as the brides of Christ. The first group consisted of the five wise virgins. They were committed to God, went to church regularly, said yes to their calling, lived according to the Word of God and kept His commandments. They believed the scripture that says that no man will know when Christ, the bridegroom will return, for his bride, the church. Because of their commitment to God they will be ready when He comes.

The second group consisted of the five foolish virgins. They attend church infrequently and believe more highly in themselves than they do God. This group is still operating according to the world's system. They are arrogant enough to believe that they will know when Christ will return for his church and will prepare themselves at that time. Because they are foolish they will not be ready when Jesus returns and will not be able to enter the kingdom of heaven. Therefore heed the warning in verse thirteen.

---

2. Read verses 15 - 30. What does this parable mean to you?

Answer: You shall reap what you sow (26)

3. If you do not give to others what is your fate? (29-30)

Sheep represent Christians, Jesus is our shepherd, and goats represent sinners.

4. How will the Son of Man come? (31)

5. How will He separate the nations? (32)

6. Who will Jesus sit on his right hand and on his left hand? (33)

7. Explain why the Christians will inherit the kingdom? (34-36)

8. What will happen to the sinners? (41)

9. What will happen to those who are only concerned about God but will not help others? (45-46)

Chapter 26 – The Last Supper, Denial, And Betrayal
1. What will happen after the Feast of Passover? (2)

2. What did the people conspire at the palace of Caiaphas? (3-4)

3. Who's house was Jesus in at Bethany? (6)

4. Describe what the woman did to Jesus at dinner? (7)

5. Why were his disciples upset at her actions? (8-9)

6. What did the oil represent? (10, 12)

7. How did this action memorialize the woman? (13)

8. Which disciple betrayed Jesus and what was he paid? (14-15)

9. What did Jesus tell the disciples at the Passover? (21, 23, 24)

10. Describe how communion took place. (26 - 28)

    This is where the Christian church learned how to take communion which is also referred to as the Lord's Supper.

11. Who was going to deny Jesus three times? (33-34)

12. How did the disciples respond? (35)

13. What did Jesus do in Gethsemane, who did He take with Him and what did He say? (36-38)

14. What did Jesus pray? (39, 42)

15. How many times did Jesus leave his disciples to pray and what did he tell them afterwards? (45, 46,)

16. How was Jesus betrayed? (48)

17. Why didn't Jesus cry unto God the Father for help? (53-54)

18. How many disciples forsook Jesus? (56)

19. Explain what happened to Peter after Jesus was accused? (69-75)

Chapter 27 – Blood Money, Crucifixion, And Burial

1. What did the chief priests and elders decide to do about Jesus and how did they send him to Pontius Pilate? (1-2)

2. How did this effect Judas? (3-5)

3. Why weren't the 30 pieces of silver put back into the treasury and what did they do with it? (6-8)

4. Who first prophesied the above event? (9)

5. How did Jesus defend himself against all the accusations? (11-14)

6. The chief priest and elders persuaded the people to crucify Jesus. How did Pilate react to this? (20, 24)

7. After Barabas was released what happened to Jesus? (26-31)

8. Who carried Jesus' cross to the hill of Golgotha? (32-33)

9. What was Jesus given to drink? (34)

10. What happened to His clothes? (35)

11. How was Jesus mocked in this hour? (37 - 43)

12. How long was there darkness upon the land? (45)

13. At the ninth hour what did Jesus cry aloud? (46)

14. What did the people say and what happened next? (46-51)

15. What happened to some of the bodies of the saints? (52)

16. Why did some say that truly Jesus was the Son of God? (51-53)

17. Name some of the women that were present at the crucifixion? (56)

18. Who asked Pilate for the body of Jesus? (57)

19. What did Josef do with the body and how did he prepare the tomb? (58-59)

20. Why did the chief priest want a guard on Jesus' tomb? (63-64)

SUMMARY

During the birth of Jesus, his father Joseph watched over his newborn infant. He was born without deformity and perfect in every way, as He laid in a dirty manger wrapped in unclean swaddling clothes (Luke 2:4). This was not a place fit for the King of Kings.

After Jesus died a physical death another man named Joseph took Jesus' beaten and defiled body and wrapped it in clean linen. He laid his body in a clean tomb. This was not a death and burial that was fit for the King of Kings, but a necessary one.

Chapter 28 – He Is Risen

1. What did the two women named Mary do at the end of the Sabbath? (1)

2. What happened when they arrived there? (2-4)

3. What did the angel of the Lord say to them? (5-7)

4. How did the women react when they saw Jesus and what did he tell them to do? (9-10)

5. What was commonly said among the Jews about Jesus not being in the tomb? (13)

6. Where did the disciples meet Jesus and what were his directives? (16 - 20)

SUMMARY QUESTIONS

1. Have you ever lied under oath? If yes what were the consequences. (72)

2. Did you ever betray a close friend or colleague? (4) How can you rectify the situation now? Suggestions: Repent for your transgressions to Jesus, and ask for forgiveness. Forgive yourself and ask the other person to forgive you.

3. Are you guilty of buying things with blood money? What is the Lord speaking to you now?

4. Were you ever in a situation where it was better for you not to say anything? Did you comply? (12-14)

5. Have you ever compromised your integrity to conform to the group consensus? What was the outcome of your actions? Is the blood on your hands? (24)

6. Has an angel of the Lord ever spoken to you? What did he/she say? (2)

7. Has there ever been a period of time when you did not hear from the Lord? You tried to speak to Him in your usual way but you could not find Him? (6) How did the Lord change your communication style and was this an opportunity for spiritual growth?

8. Are you keeping a lie alive? (12-13) What is it? What does the Lord want you to do about it?

9. Are you the firstborn child? If so what is required of you according to your culture's traditions? What is God requiring of you?

$\mathcal{T}$HE BOOK OF DANIEL

Step Nine: Do Not Be Deceived God Is Not Mocked For Whatsoever A Man Soweth, That Shall He Also Reap

Daniel was one of the Major Prophets and seers of the Bible. As mentioned in the Book of Ezekiel, Daniel was known for his righteousness and wisdom (Ezekiel 14:14, 20; 28:3) and many biblical historians believe that Daniel was of royal birth as written in chapter 1:3, 4, 6. In Matthew 24:15, Mark 13:14, Jesus quoted the prophecies of Daniel.

When you get to Chapter 9 in the book of Daniel you will notice that many of the scriptures are mentioned in the book of Revelation. Daniel was a prophet that was given a vision of the end-times.

In this step you will write about Daniel and yourself at the same time. God has something in store for you as you complete this step.

Chapter 1 – Name Changes

1. Who was Nebuchadnezzar? (1)

2. What kind of children were chosen for the king's palace and what was there purpose? (4)

3. What did their diet consist of and for how long? (5)

4. What names did the Prince of the Eunuchs give the Hebrew boys? (7)

5. What is your given name? Are you being called by a name that is not pleasing to God?

6. What did Daniel decide to do about the king's diet? (8, 12, 13)

7. How did the prince of the Eunuchs respond? (10)

8. What was observed and how did they compare to the others who are the king's diet? (15)

9. What does your diet consist of? Is the Lord calling you to fast for 10 days or more?

10. What gifts did the Lord give the four children? (17)

11. What did the king think of them? (20)

12. What types of gifts do you possess and what do others think about you?

Chapter 2 - Dreams

1. What type of dreams did Nebuchadnezzar have and how did they affect him? (1)

2. Do you suffer from night mares and an interrupted sleep cycle?

3. What did the king command? (2,3)

4. Have you ever turned to astrology, palm reading, etc. for insight into your inner most being? If so what were the consequences?

5. What was the unreasonable demand that was spoken by the king? (5, 12)

6. Has anyone ever made an unreasonable demand of you? If so, explain.

7. How did the children answer? (10, 11)

8. Summarize how Daniel handled the decree. (14-18)

9. When and how was the secret revealed to Daniel? (19)

10. Explain the last time the Lord revealed something to you in a vision or a dream.

11. What did Daniel tell Nebuchadnezzar and how he received the interpretation of his dream? (27)

12. What did Daniel proclaim about God? (20–23)

13. (Read verse 27) Do you know of any government leaders, now or in the past, that have contacted astrologers, palm readers, and/or psychics for advice?

14. Read the interpretation of the king's dream. (37-45)

15. What is talked about in verse 44, has this been fulfilled?

16. How did the king reward Daniel and what did he say about his God? (46-48)

17. Did Daniel forget about his friends once he was promoted? (49)

What about you, did your friendships change after a job promotion?

Chapter 3 – Tradition And Idols

1. Why did King Nebchadnezzer call all of the heads of government into Babylon? (1-2)

2. What instructions were given about the images? (4-5)

3. Have you ever been pressured to do something because of tradition or because it was expected or insisted by a manager that was contrary to the word of God?

4. What did the Chaldeans say about Shadrach, Meshach and Abednego? (8, 12)

5. How did they respond to the accusations? (17, 18)

6. Were you ever confronted for holding fast to your religious beliefs? Explain

7. Were you reprimanded in any way?

8. What was the punishment for disobeying the king? (19-23)

9. What did the king observe? (24, 25)

10. (Read verses 25-26) Isn't it ironic that even though the king was worshiping idols he was very much aware of who the one true living God is.

11. Did you ever live like this, acknowledging God only when you were in a crisis? When things are going well you tended to put God on the back burner.

12. What did the king decree? (29)

13. Have you ever influenced a change in your neighborhood, workplace, or school because the people around you saw the Christ in you?

Chapter 4 – Dreams And Visions

1. (Read verses 1-18) Nebuchadnezzar had another vision. Again he went back to his old way of doing things the moment he got stressed. He called for the magicians, astrologers, and soothsayers. When they were unable to help, then the king called on the prophet of the most High God.

2. Did you ever have a dream or vision that you did not understand?

3. Did a series of events happen in your life that you believed were there to teach you a life lesson but you had no interpretation there of? Who did you call first? Who did you call last?

4. How did Daniel interpret the king's dream? (24-26)

5. Why did Daniel beg the king to stop sinning? (27)

6. Did anyone ever beg you to stop sinning? What were you involved in and what were the consequences?

7. What happened to the king after 12 months? (29-33)

8. Explain the king's epiphany? (34-37)

Chapter 5 – Handwriting On The Wall

1. Who was Belshazzar and what kind of feast did he have? (1-4)

2. Why did the king's countenance change? (5-6)

3. Who did he ask for and were they helpful? (7-8)

4. What did his queen suggest? (10-11)

5. What did Daniel tell Belshazzar about his father? (17-21)

6. What did Daniel tell Belshazzar about himself? (22-23)

7. Has anyone ever confronted you about your family and if so for what purpose?

8. What was the interpretation of the dream? (24-29)

9. What happened to Belteshazzar? (30)

10. What proclamation was made about Daniel? (29)

11. Who took over the kingdom? (31)

Chapter 6 – The Lion's Den

1. Daniel was the first (head) over three presidents, why was he preferred over the others? (3)

2. The other presidents and princes conspired against Daniel. What did they get the king to decree? (6-9)

3. What action did Daniel take when he knew the decree had been signed? (10)

4. What action did the king take to enforce his decree? (16-17)

5. The king went to see if Daniel survived the lion's den. What did he find out? (20-22)

6. Were you ever thrown under the bus by people you worked for? Did you survive the attack or did you have to find another job and start over?

7. What did the king do to Daniel's accusers? (24)

8. What was the new decree and what did it say about God? (26-27)

Chapter 7 – Daniel's Vision

1. In the first year of Belshazzar, Daniel had a dream and visions. Read verses 1-12 and make an interpretation if you can with help from the symbolic meanings of the following words:

   Lion - rulership or royal authority
   Eagle - spiritual or divine omniscience and victory
   Horns - force, strength, virility, and combat
   Wings - sign of elevation or protection
   Bear - cold blooded brutality and savagery
   Leopard - cruel, ruthless and powerful in exploits and conquests
   Second or Two - covenant, mutuality or accord
   Ten - God's divine law
   Four - worldwide impact
   Son of Man - Jesus

Ram - power and virility

Goat - cruelty, brutality, a demonic symbol, Satan

Gabriel - the messenger archangel

2. The interpretation of the vision is described in verses 13-27. Is this about the past, present, or future? Explain

3. Now go back to the book of Revelation and reinterpret this chapter in Daniel according to Revelation 1:7, 17; 11:15b, and 13:1-8. It is likely that you have received another revelation about the future.

Chapter 8 – The Ram And The Goat

1. Read verses 1-14.

2. What does this passage of text mean to you?

3. Gabriel explained to Daniel what will happen in later times. Summarize verses 17 - 26 and explain when the latter times will occur.

Chapter 9 - Prayer

1. Why did Daniel seek God's face through prayer and fasting? (5-14)

2. What did Daniel ask of God? (16-19)

3. What did Gabriel say to Daniel? (21-27)

   Compare this to Matthew 24:15, 24.

4. The people are given 70 weeks to end their transgression. The number seven symbolizes Divine revolutions and cycles as well as Divine Sovereignty. The number ten represents Divine economy and Divine Law. With this in mind explain the meaning of verse 24.

Chapter 10 – The River

1. In the third year of Cyrus describe what Daniel was going through? (1-4)

2. Who did Daniel see at the great river? (5-6)

3. What did the men that were with him see? (7)

4. What happened to Daniel next and what posture did he assume? (8-10)

5. What did the Angel tell him about his prayer and why it was delayed? (11-14)

6. What did Daniel do and say next? (15-17)

7. How did Daniel get strengthened and what was explained to him? (19-20)

8. There are two kingdoms at war, the kingdom of heaven and the kingdom of darkness. Where are you in the fight for your soul? Has God sent someone to you to explain your circumstances? Have you fasted and prayed for clarity? Will you?

Chapter 11 – Warring Kingdoms

1. The angel continues to explain the truth about Persia and Greece. (2) Who will make an agreement with the king of the south and the north? (6)

2. Who will prevail at the end the north or south? (7)

3. The north and the south battle for many years? (7-32) Has this happened in your own country's history? What about in other countries where inhabitants from the north fought against inhabitants from the south, what was the outcome?

4. There will be a new charismatic ruler. He will deny the one true and living God and will exhort himself. What religion is he and what is his sexual orientation? (36-37)

5. What countries will be overthrown by this nation? (42-43)

6. What will happen to end his reign? (45)

Compare Daniel 11:36-45 with Revelation 13:11-18 and make an interpretation.

Chapter 12 – The End Times

1. How will God's people be delivered? (1-3)

2. What did the Angel command Daniel to do? (4)

3. At the end of this vision what did Daniel see on each side of the river? (5-6)

4. What did the men standing on the river represent? (7)

5. Did Daniel understand his vision? (8)

6. What was to come of his vision? (9,13)

7. Draw a conclusion between Daniel 12:9 and Revelation 1:1.

SUMMARY

The Daniel fast as we know it today, consists of vegetables, fruit, and water for a specified period of time. In chapter one Daniel fasted for ten days, and in chapter ten Daniel fasted for three weeks. Is the Lord calling you to a fast? Many churches instruct their members to go on the Daniel fast once a year and that is fine. Tune into God's frequency. Your walk with God may require more fasting and praying than what you have done in the past. When Daniel needed to hear from God, he fasted and prayed. What is the Lord telling you right now?

The Bible is about the past, present, and future. As you can see, Daniel was given a vision of the end times. Were you able to see the current world events illustrated in the book of Daniel? Were you able to see the end time events? What vision has the Lord given you?

The Kingdom of Darkness is warring against the Kingdom of Heaven. It is important to seek the face of God and without relying on astrology, psychics, or palm readers to help you make decisions. After all Satan is the father of lies and he works through those mediums. He has found many ways to deceive the people of this world. We are living at the end of the age. Seek Godly counsel and all will be well with thee.

My People Perish For Lack of Knowledge
(Hosea 4:6)

CHAPTER TEN

HE BOOK OF JAMES

Step Ten: Resist Temptation

The book of James was one of the first New Testament books written and has been called the Proverbs of the New Testament. It was written by Jesus' half-brother, James who was a leader in the early Jewish Christian church. He saw Jesus after his resurrection and was with the other apostles during Pentecost. The book of James is full of wisdom, teaches faith, and shows you how to resist temptation.

Chapter 1 - Temptation

1. What should our attitude be when we fall into various temptations? (2)

2. What does the trying of our faith produce? (3)

3. If we desire wisdom what shall we do? (5)

4. Describe a double minded man. (6-8)

5. What did the Lord promise to those who endure temptation? (12)

6. Who is the tempter? (13)

7. Describe the development and the consequences of temptation. (14-15)

8. How do we obtain every good and perfect gifts? (17)

9. How were we conceived of the Father? (18)

10. How are we to speak, hear, and regulate our feelings of wrath? (20)

11. What saves our souls, how do we receive it, and what do we lay aside? (21)

12. Describe doers of the word. (20, 23, 25)

13. Can you call yourself holy and not watch what you speak? (26)

Chapter 2 – Rich And Poor, Royal Law

1. Described the difference in treatment between the rich and poor. (3, 4, 6)

2. Does this happen in our own church/life?

3. Who has chosen the poor of this world? (5)

4. What is the royal law? (8)

5. If you keep some of the commandments and not all are you guilty of committing sin? (10, 11)

6. The scripture says that faith without works is dead. (20, 29)

   Read verses 14-18 and explain the message.

7. How did Abraham and Rahab prove their faith in God? (21-25)

> Being obedient to God as well as believing the promises of God is a true testament of your faith.

Chapter 3 – Power of The Tongue

There is power in the spoken word. If you continue to speak something eventually it will come to pass. (5)

1. If we put bits in the horses' mouth to control their whole bodies, what say ye about your mouth and your body? (2, 3)

2. Describe the power of the tongue. (2-8)

3. What kind of contradictory statements do we as humans make? (9, 10)

4. How do you open yourself up to demonic influences? (14, 16)

5. How do we distinguish wisdom that comes from the most High God and wisdom that does not? (17-18)

Chapter 4 – Worldly Things

1. What kind of relationship do you have with God if you are consumed with the lusts of the world? (4)

2. What is another way to depart from evil? (7, 8, 11)

3. Who is the highest law giver? (12)

4. What does the scripture say about humility? (6, 10)

5. What is human life like and can we predict what will happen tomorrow? (14)

Chapter 5 – Advice To The Brethren

1. Describe the actions of some ungodly rich men. (1-6)

2. What should be done for the afflicted and the sick? (13-14)

3. How powerful is prayer? (15-18)

4. Describe the fate of sinners. (15, 20)

These are the instructions about how to resist temptation. If you are struggling with any type of compulsive or immoral behavior pray these verses as often as needed and follow their directives.

RESIST TEMPTATION

- Let every man be swift to hear, slow to speak, slow to wrath. (1:19)
- Lay apart all filthiness and superfluity of naughtiness and receive with meekness the engrafted word which is able to save your souls. (1:21)
- Be ye doers of the word and not hearers only, deceiving your own selves. (1:22)
- Thou shall love thy neighbor as thy self. (2:8)
- There is one God. (2:19)
- Speak blessings not curses. (3:10)
- Seek wisdom from above. (3:17)
- Submit yourselves to God. Resist the devil and he will flee from you. (4:7)
- Draw nigh to God and he will draw nigh to you. (4:8)
- Cleanse your hands ye sinners and purify your hearts ye double minded. (4:8)
- Humble yourselves in the sight of the Lord, and He shall lift you up. (4:10)
- Speak not evil one of another. (4:11)
- Do not give in to the lust of the flesh (4:1-5)
- Confess your faults one to another. (5:16)
- Forgive (5:15)

$\mathcal{T}$HE BOOK OF PHILLIPPIANS

Step Eleven: Be Thankful, Rejoice, And Live In Peace

The Apostle Paul wrote this epistle to the Phillippians. The church at Phillipi was established on Paul's second missionary trip and his first trip on European soil. This church supported him and sent him money when he was in Thessalonica, Corinth, and Rome. In this epistle Paul continues to uplift this congregation, exhort, and instruct them in the way of the Lord.

Chapter 1 – Suffering And Affliction

1. Do you often get discouraged and want to give up because the promise of God for your life has not yet manifested?

2. Think about someone else who is down and discouraged, pray verses 2, 3, 4, 9, and 11 over them.

3. Paul suffered many things in his life, how was his suffering used? (12, 13)

4. How was Paul's afflictions used by other ministers in the gospel? (13. 14)

5. Paul wrote that his imprisonment has affected the preaching of the gospel in two ways, explain. (15-17)

6. How did the preaching of others effect Paul? (18-25)

7. What is proved if you are not terrified by your adversaries? (28)

8. Are Christians likely to suffer in many of the ways Jesus did? (29)

Chapter 2 – Be Like Jesus

1. What attitude and behavior should believers exhibit? (2-5)

2. Describe why and how Jesus was sent to earth? (6-8)

3. Describe the attributes of the name of Jesus? (9-10)

4. What should every tongue confess? (11)

5. How should we do all good things? (14)

6. What should be represented in us? (15)

7. When you are serving Christ know that there will be set backs and attacks. What should our attitudes be when this happens? (16)

Chapters 3 & 4 – Christian Living

1. How do we worship God? (3:3)

2. How does Paul describe himself? (3:5)

3. Who did he persecute in his early life? (3:6)

4. How does Paul feel about the things he had to give up for Jesus to preach the gospel? (3:7-8)

5. Where does righteousness come from? (3:9)

6. What should our mind set be if we are to follow Christ? (3:13, 3:14, 4:4, 4:13)

7. An intimate relationship with the Lord should reveal the following: (3:10, 3:20, 3:21, 4:8)

8. How do we make our request know to God? (4:6)

9. What should the peace of God do? (4:7, 4:9, 4:11, 4:19)

SUMMARY

The book of Phillipians is a short book that is packed with power and might. This book will be instrumental in changing negative mind-sets. The verses have been grouped according to the categories of thanksgiving, joy, and peace.

BE THANKFUL FOR WHO YOU ARE IN CHRIST

- I thank my God for your fellowship in the gospel (1:3, 5)
  According to my earnest expectation and my hope that in nothing I shall be ashamed but that with all boldness, as always, so now also Christ shall be magnified in my body whether it be life or death (1:20)
- For unto you it is given in the behalf of Christ not only to believe on him but also to suffer for his sake (1:29)
- I can do all things through Christ which strengthens me (4:13)
- Brethren this one thing I do, forgetting those things which are behind and reaching forth unto those things which are before. (3:13)
- I press toward the mark for the prize of the high calling of God in Christ Jesus (3:14)
  Whatsoever things are true, whatsoever things are honest, whatsoever things are just, whatsoever things are lovely, whatsoever things are of a good report, if there be any virtue, and if there be any praise, think on these things. (4:8)
- In everything by prayer and supplication with thanksgiving let your requests be made known unto God (4:6)

REJOICE

- Always in every prayer make requests with joy (1:4)
- Whether in pretense or in truth Christ is preached and I therein do rejoice! (1:18)
- Your rejoicing is more abundant in Jesus Christ (1:26) and I pray that your love may abound yet more and more in knowledge and in all discernment (1:9)
- Worship God in the spirit and rejoice in Christ Jesus and have no confidence in the flesh (3:3)
- Holding forth the word of life that I may rejoice in the day of Christ, that I have not run in vain, neither labored in vain (2:16)
- For I have learned in whatsoever state I am, that I will be content (4:11). My brethren, rejoice in the Lord! (3:1)

PEACE

- Grace be unto you and peace from God our Father and the Lord Jesus Christ (1:2)
- Do all things without murmurings and disputing (2:14)
- Let this mind be in you which is also in Christ Jesus (2:5)
- Those things which ye have both learned and received and heard and seen in me do, and the God of peace shall be with you (4:9)
- My God shall supply all your need according to his riches in glory by Christ Jesus (4:19)
- And the peace of God which passeth all understanding shall keep your hearts and minds through Christ Jesus (4:7)

No Matter The Circumstances
BE THANKFUL, REJOICE, AND LIVE IN PEACE

CHAPTER TWELVE

THE BOOK OF JOB

Step Twelve: Seek The Lord And Do Not Look Back

This book is written about Job but the author is unknown. Some historians say that Job wrote part of it while others credit Moses for the authorship. This book describes the tragedy of Job and his family. Many Christians disagree with the reason why this happened to him, but we can all agree that suffering is part of the human condition. We live in a world that is dominated by Satan brought on by the fall of man, through Adam.

I have reordered the way in which you read the chapters. For those of you who have read the book of Job before, this will give you new insight into what he was saying, as well as his friends, and most importantly what God is saying.

Chapter 1- Job And His Children

1. What kind of man was Job? (1)

2. How many children did he have? (2)

3. Describe his wealth (3)

4. How did his sons feast? (4)

5. Why did Job offer burnt offerings on behalf of his sons? (5)

6. What did the Lord think about Job? (8)

7. How did Satan describe Job? (10)

8. Why was Satan unable to torment Job? (10)

9. What did Satan want God to do? (11)

10. How did God respond? (12)

11. Where were his children eating and drinking and what happened to them? (13, 18, 19)

12. What happened to Job's livestock? (14-17)

13. How did Job respond to the bad news? (20-22)

Chapter 2 – Job Is Afflicted

1. What did God allow Satan to do concerning Job? (4-7)

2. What did Job's wife tell him to do after his afflictions? (9)

3. How did Job respond? (10)

4. Who were Job's friends and why did they come to see him? (11)

5. How did his friends respond when they saw him? (12)

6. How many days did Job's friend spend with him and why did they not speak? (13)

Instructions: Now read the rest of Job to get a general understanding. When you are through you may proceed with the remaining questions. The remaining study questions are grouped according to what is said by Job, his friends, and by what God has to say in the last chapters.

Chapters 15 -41 will make more sense to you if you read each chapter beginning at the last verse to the first verse, in reverse order.

JOB SPEAKS TEN TIMES
First Discourse
Chapter 3- Job Curses His Birth

1. What did Job say about his life and birth? (1-9)

2. Why do you think that Job begins to curse the day he was born? (10-13)

3. What did he say about suffering people? (20-23)

4. What was Job concerned about? (25-26)

Job was always in fear. As we learned in Part I, Step 8, fear has torment. Thoughts are seeds. If you think about something long enough eventually those seeds will sprout and manifest in your life.

Second Discourse
Chapter 6 – Sadness and Despair
Job answers Eliphaz.

1. How does Job describe his grief? (2,3)

2. Why was Job unable to communicate for several days? (3)

3. Who does he blame for his misfortune? (4)

4. Does Job want to live or die? (9-11), (7:15)

5. Does Job understand why this has happened to him? (23,24)

Chapter 7 – Pain and Suffering
1. Job is wallowing in his sorrow. How does he describe himself? (5-9)

2. How is Job sleeping? (3, 4, 14)

3. Have you ever suffered through something that was so painful that you wanted to die?

4. When you were going through your trial did you believe that you did something to cause your pain?

5. While Job is suffering he doesn't believe that he will ever come out of this. When you were in the midst of a trial did you have similar thoughts?

Third Discourse
Chapter 9 - Grief
1. How does Job describe God? (4-11)

2. How is Job feeling condemned by God? (16-17)

3. According to Job, who does God destroy? (22)

4. Why is Job afraid to let go his grief? (27-28)

Chapter 10 - Confusion
1. What does Job say about his soul? (1)

2. What will Job say to God? (2)

3. Why is Job perplexed about what is happening in his life? (7)

4. How does Job remind God of his humanness? (9, 11, 12, 18-22)

5. Job wonders if God can see things through human eyes. (4, 15)

6. Job reminds God that he is afflicting him. (6,7, 10, 14, 16, 17)

Fourth Discourse
Chapter 12 - Dejection

1. Explain how Job felt that his friends were putting him down. (2,3)

2. Explain how Job feels ashamed and that he is being mocked. (4)

3. How are those that are in sin living according to Job? (6)

4. Job talks about the mightiness of God, summarize. (7-25)

Chapter 13 – Wallowing in Grief

1. Explain how Job continues to disagree with his friends about how he should handle his grief and the reason he is in that situation. (1-12)

2. How does Job want to wallow in his grief? (13)

3. What does Job say about trust? (15, 16)

4. What does Job believe will happen to him if he is not allowed to plead his case? (19)

5. What are the two things Job ask of God? (21)

Chapter 14 – Life and Death

1. What does Job say about the length of the lifespan? (1,2,5)

2. Is there life after death? (10, 11, 12, 14)

Fifth Discourse

Chapter 16 – Tears and Sorrow

1. What does Job believe that will happen to him in a few years? (22)

2. How does Job want to communicate with God? (21)

3. Describe how Job cries unto God even though his friends don't understand. (20)

4. Job continues to mourn, describe. (15,16)

5. Why does Job believe that God is punishing him? (11-14)

6. What does Job say about his friends and their ability to comfort him in his time of need? (1)

Chapter 17 – Doom and Gloom

1. Describe how Job continues to complain and speak of his impending doom? (1-16)

2. What does Job accuse his friends of? (10)

Sixth Discourse
Chapter 19 - Blaming

1. How many times was Job reproached? (3)

2. How does Job continue to blame God for his misfortune? (6-12)

3. Who has deserted Job? (13,14)

4. Even though Job is afflicted what is he convinced of? (25)

Seventh Discourse
Chapter 21 – The Wicked

1. Who is Job complaining to? (1-4)

2. He talks about how the wicked are doing well, what else can you summarize from this chapter.

Eighth Discourse
Chapter 23 & 24
Summarize these two chapters in which Job declares that he has been obedient to God and talks about those who do not know God.

Ninth Discourse
This lengthy discourse includes chapters 26-31. Add to the summaries already given.

Chapter 26
Job talks about God.

Chapter 27
Job pledges his allegiance to God and talks about Him.

Chapter 28
He continues to talk about God. What is wisdom and understanding according to Job 28:28

Chapter 29
Job talked about how God preserved him.

Chapter 30
Job talks about his pain again.

Chapter 31
Job compares his life to those who sin, and stated that if he lived an unholy life then what has happened to him would be justified.

SUMMARY OF JOB'S DISCOURSE
Clinically speaking, Job was suffering from depression. He lost hope, had terrifying dreams and vision, suffered from insomnia and suicidal ideation, but had not orchestrated a plan to take his life, but expressed a desire to die. He was sad and despondent and did not speak for seven days. According to Job, God does not discriminate when it comes to whom He

will destroy, the righteous or the wicked. He did not understand why this has happened in his life and took no consolation from his friends.

Tenth Discourse
Chapter 42
Job admits to God that he has heard of Him but has never seen Him until now. Then Job repents.

The Five Tragedies of Job
List the five tragedies of Job as found in the following verses.

1. (1:15)   4. (1:19)
2. (1:16)   5. (2:7)
3. (1:17)

ELIPHAZ SPEAKS THREE TIMES
First Discourse
Chapter 4 –Handling Your Own Crisis
1. What did Eliphaz the Temanite ask Job? (2)

2. How did Job respond to others in their time of need? (3, 4)

3. How is Job handling his own crisis according to Eliphaz? (5,6)

4. What does verse eight mean to you?

5. Is Eliphaz accusing Job of bringing this affliction upon himself? (7,8,9)

6. What is Eliphaz's view of God and mortal man? (17-21)

Chapter 5 – What to Expect

In this chapter Eliphaz continues to counsel and question Job.

1. What does wrath and envy do to man? (2)

2. What happened to the children of the foolish? (4,5)

3. Because man is born into trouble what should he do? (8)

4. What can be expected from God? (9, 10)

5. How does God provide for the poor? (15, 16)

6. How does God handle the crafty and the wise? (12-14)

7. Why should we trust in the Lord? (17, 18)

8. What good things are going to come out this according to Eliphaz? (19-26)

Second Discourse
Chapter 15 – Hot Air

1. What does Eliphaz think of Job's lengthy tirade? (1-6)

2. What else does Eliphaz convey to Job about his way of thinking? (7-14)

3. How does Eliphaz describe the life of the wicked? (15-35)

Third Discourse
Chapter 22 – Decree A Thing

1. What did Eliphaz accuse Job of? (5-9)

2. Why does Eliphaz implore Job to return back to God? (21-27)

3. Why should Job decree a thing? (28)

SUMMARY OF ELIPHAZ'S DISCOURSE

It is Eliphaz's belief that you reap what you sow. He has a pessimistic view of human nature stating that men are born into trouble. He wants Job to admit his guilt and chastening of the Lord so that he can go on with his life. Eliphaz told Job that he has helped many people that were down and out but now that it has happened to him he is unable to cope. Eliphaz prophesied to Job and said that he would live a long life with many offspring. He then contradicts himself and accuses Job of not helping those in need. Eliphaz's advice is driven by his emotions and personal opinion.

BILDAD SPEAKS THREE TIMES
First Discourse
Chapter 8 – More Hot Air

In this chapter Bildad the Shuhite is tired of Job's pessimism and answers Job's lament.

1. How does Bildad describe Job's tirade? (2)

2. How does Bildad tell Job to change his behavior? (5)

3. What did Bildad prophecy to Job? (7)

4. For those who forget God and are hypocritical what will happen to their hope and trust? (13,14).

5. What can be expected from God? (20)

6. What will happen to the wicked and the hateful? (22)

Second Discourse
Chapter 18 - Confrontation
1. Bildad confronts Job about his attitude and what he thinks of his friends and their advice. (1-3)

2. Describe what Bildad said will happen to the wicked and those who do not know God. (5-19)

Third Discourse
Chapter 25
1. How does Bildad describe man in God's eyes? (1-6)

SUMMARY OF BILDAD'S DISCOURSE
Bildad complains that Job is not taking the advice of the elders. He said that no man that is born of a woman is clean. It is his belief that Job is suffering and his children were killed because they sinned. He prophesied to Job and said that his later days would be greater than his former. Even though Bildad held a pessimistic view as well, God used him to speak life into Job with a prophetic word.

ZOPHAR SPEAKS TWO TIMES
First Discourse
Chapter 11 – Guilty As Charged

1. What does Zophar the Naamathite think about Job's last tirade? (3)

2. Does Zophar believe that Job is as innocent as he proclaims to be? (4)

3. What is Zophar telling Job about God? (7-10)

4. How is Job instructed to seek God? (13-15)

5. What did Zophar tell Job to do with his misery? (16)

6. What words of encouragement was he given? (17-19)

7. What will happen to the wicked according to Zophar? (20)

Second Discourse
Chapter 20 – Hypocrites and The Wicked

1. How long do the hypocrites and wicked enjoy their sin? (5)

2. Summarize the life and fate of the wicked. (7-29)

SUMMARY OF ZOPHAR'S DISCOURSE

Zophar agrees with his two friends and believed Job sinned. He shows no compassion and stated that Job received less than what he deserved. Zophar has a one-sided view of humanity and is over-focused on what the wicked do. He has lost sight of true friendship and does not offer a blessing or a prophetic word.

ELIHU SPEAKS ONCE
Discourse
Chapter 32 – A New Perspective

1. Why did Job's three friends stop speaking? (1)

2. What was Elihu angry about? (2-3)

3. Why did Elihu wait to speak? (4)

4. What did Elihu say about age and wisdom concerning the three who spoke before him? (7-9)

5. How is Elihu going to express himself? (17-22)

Chapter 33 - Instructions

1. What instructions did Elihu give Job? (1)

2. How does Elihu describe himself? (2-7)

3. Elihu tells Job how he can hear from God? (14-16)

4. What does Elihu tell Job about God? (17-30)

Chapter 34 – Characteristics Of God

1. According to Elihu what kind of God do we serve? (12)

2. Can evil men hide from God? (22)

3. What did Elihu say about Job in verses 35-37?

Chapter 35 – The Oppressed

1. Does God hear vanity? (13)

2. What and how do the oppress cry out? (9-12)

Chapter 36 & 37 – About God

1. Who does Elihu speak for?

2. What is Elihu describing by using a series of questions?

SUMMARY OF ELIHU'S DISCOURSE

Elihu had better insight into Job's situation. He stated that the righteous nor the wicked effect who God is, because He is sovereign. Elihu goes on to say that great men are not always wise and that God does not commit iniquity. Elihu was aware that the god of this world brings death and destruction in his attempt to destroy the inhabitants of the earth.

THE LORD SPEAKS TO JOB
Discourse
The Lord answers Job with a series of questions that depicts his omnipotent power.

Chapter 38
1. How did the Lord manifest his presence to Job? (1)

2. What is the Lord saying to Job with this series of questions? (2-41)

Chapter 39
1. If the Lord was speaking these words to you instead of Job, what would your reaction be?

Chapter 40
1. How did god challenge Job? (1-12)

Chapter 41
1. What is the message in this chapter?

THE LORD SPEAKS TO ELIPHAZ
Discourse
Chapter 42
1. Why was God angry? (7)

2. What did the Lord instruct Eliphaz and his friends to do, and did they comply? (8, 9)

3. What did the Lord do after Job prayed? (10)

LESSONS LEARNED

God taught everyone involved in this tragedy a lesson, even Satan. The three older men found out that bad things really do happen to good people. None of them were able to offer Job positive coping strategies. Their lack of compassion and insight to a hurting friend angered God and required repentance and sacrifice. Elihu knew that Job's tragedy did not come from God, but from Satan. Satan learned that he harms those who God allows.

Elihu also stated that the Spirit in man brings wisdom, not age. Job learned that tears and self-pity do not move God. Faith and repentance move God. Because of the tragedies that Job experienced, he developed a closer relationship with the Lord. Job did not curse God and remained faithful to Him. The Lord rewarded him by restoring everything he lost two-fold.

The scriptures reveal that Job lived 210 years. Although it is not written in the book of Job, we can assume that after this tragedy, he had a powerful testimony. Because of his wealth and influence in his community Job had the opportunity to affect positive change for four generations. He had the ability to offer others hope, faith, belief in God, and a willingness to press through the pain. Difficult times are not fun or pleasant but they afford us the opportunity to develop a closer relationship with God. It is the way the Lord chooses to stretch us and to mature us, as we are elevated in our calling in the kingdom of God.

CHARTS AND SUMMARY OF JOB'S LIFE
THE FIVE TRAGEDIES OF JOB
First Tragedy (1:15)
*   His oxen and donkeys were stolen by the Sabeans and the servants were killed

Second Tragedy (1:16)
*   The fire of God fell from heaven, his sheep were burned and his servants killed

Third Tragedy (1:17)
*   The Chaldeans stole his camels and killed his servants

Fourth Tragedy (1:19)

- A great wind blew down the houses with his sons and daughters in them, and all men were killed

Fifth Tragedy (2:7)

- Job developed boils from the top of his head to soles of his feet
  After the fifth tragedy Job was given grace.

JOB'S LIFE

Before The Tragedies	After The Tragedies
7 sons and 3 daughters	7 sons and 3 daughters (Plus 4 generations)
Age 70	Age 70 + 140 = 210
7,000 sheep	14,000 sheep
3,000 camels	6,000 camels
500 oxen	1,000 oxen
500 donkeys	1,000 donkeys
He offered burnt offerings for his children who did not seek God for themselves, sinned, did not repent, and died at the hand of Satan	He offered one burnt offerings for his friends, Job repented, prayed for his friends and received restoration, wholeness, and multiplication in family and possessions

Meaning of Names In The Book Of Job

Job - persecuted one, to come back, to repent

Jemima - a specified time, a hot day

Kezia - to strip off, scrape, corner

Kerenhappuch - a horn, a flask, to paint, to dye (cosmetics)

Eliphaz - God of gold

Bildad – confusing love

Zophar - to return, depart early

Elihu - he is my God

Sabeans - descendants of Sheba, Ethiopians

Sheba - seven or oath

Chaldeans - the wisest people of that region, clod-breakers
Clod - a lump or chunk, an ignorant person
(Strong, 1990; Webster, 1998)

Job's life can be summarized using the meaning of the names of a few people in his life. This is a brief example of the living Bible, the Word of God with its many layers and dimensions that are revealed to you as you study the Word of God. Highlight or underline the definition of the names as you read the following synopsis.

Job was a good man but Satan was allowed to persecute him, for a specified time, because there was a legal opening called fear. Job continually offered burnt offerings for his children because they sinned, cursed God, and partied all of the time. Even when Job developed boils that he scraped from his body, he never took an oath against God. His wife wanted him to curse God and die. However, Job did not confuse his love for his wife with his love for God.

Job's friends, considered some of the wisest in the land came to console him. But in the midst of his despair he did not speak to them for seven days. God sent a prophet, named Elihu, to speak for Him. Elihu said that Job's friends were clods and he gave Job another perspective to the tragedies he was experiencing. The Lord pulled Job through because he never turned his back on God and in the end, Job repented. The God of Gold restored his health and wealth two-fold. Job was able to return to his position of stature and influence in his family and community. His daughters adorned themselves with cosmetics and were considered the fairest in the land.

Unlike Job, you don't need burnt offerings to atone for your sins or your children's sins. Jesus the last and final sacrifice makes intercession for us, and by grace are we saved. In order for you to see the fullness of God manifest in your life it will be necessary for you to repent and turn from your wicked ways. If your children or other family members are lost in sin, don't give God a burnt offering for them, instead intercede for them through prayer and fasting.

Job was limited in what he could do for his children. Unlike Job, you have more resources available to you in God the Father, Jesus the Son of God, the Holy Spirit, and the Holy Bible. They were given to us so that we may have life and have it more abundantly (see John 10:10).

SUMMARY QUESTIONS

1. Many of you have already experienced many tragedies in your life, just like Job. At that time were you sad, depressed, and despondent?

2. Did you lose hope, isolate, and refuse to talk to your friends?

3. Was your body disfigured by an accident or a disease?

4. Now that you have worked through the 12 steps, describe how God restored what you lost?

5. Was there a two-fold or greater return on your loss?

6. What was the root cause of your affliction(s)?

CONCLUSION

$\mathcal{W}$ALK THIS WAY

By now the people closest to you have noticed a change in you, they see the Christ in you. When they ask about your transformation, tell them that the Lord God Almighty has ordered your steps and there are only twelve of them!

These are the twelve steps to staying free.

Step One	Say the Name
Step Two	Confess that Jesus is the Son of God
Step Three	Repent
Step Four	Forgive
Step Five	Pray

Collectively, Steps 1-5 lead to Step 6.

Step Six	Deliverance from strongholds

If you say the name of Jesus, confess that He is the Son of God, repent for your sins, forgive those who have hurt you, pray without ceasing, then the Lord, God almighty will deliver you from your afflictions.

He shall deliver thee in six troubles, yea in seven there shall no evil touch thee (Job 5:19).

Steps 7 - 12 show the battle we are in on a daily basis, the battle between good and evil. Follow these steps to defeat the forces of evil unto victory.

Evil	Good
Step Seven - Rebuke Satan	Step Eight - Submit to God
Step Nine - Don't let Satan deceive you	Step Eleven - Thank the Lord
Step Ten - Resist Satan	Step Twelve - Seek the Lord

By completing *Seek Ye First The Kingdom Of God*, like Job, you have told your story. You have overcome through repentance, forgiveness, and by the Word of the most High God. While you were lost in the quagmire of despair, God sent someone to speak life into your soul, and in the midst of it, God himself showed up.

• *Now that you have been delivered and set free when will you share these steps with others so that they can experience the goodness of God?*

THE 12 STEP MANDATE
Be ye not ashamed of the Gospel of Christ (Romans 1:16a) and go into all the world and preach the gospel to every creature (Mark 16:15). Repentance and remission of sins should also be preached in His name to all nations (Luke 24:47), confirming the Word with signs following (Mark 16:20). Because it is the power of God unto salvation to everyone that believeth (Romans 1:16). Whosoever findeth Christ, findeth life (Proverbs 8:35), and he that believeth not shall be damned (Mark 16:16b). Be not weary in well doing (Galatians 6:9) because you can do all things through Christ who strengthens you (Phillippians 4:13).

PROVERBIAL PRAYER

God is a shield unto them that put their trust in Him (30:5). Therefore I will trust in the Lord with all my heart and lean not unto my own understanding because the fear of the Lord is the beginning of wisdom (9:10), and understanding is a wellspring of life (16:22).

I will keep God's commandments for length of days and long life and peace shall they add to me (3:1-2). I will keep my heart with all diligence for out of it are the issues of life (4:23). Every word of God is pure (30:5). Death and life are in the power of the tongue (18:21).

Discretion shall preserve me and understanding shall keep me (2:11) and by mercy and truth, iniquity is purged from me (16:6).

In all my ways I will acknowledge God and He shall direct my path (3:5-6).

The Proverbial Prayer is taken from the book of Proverbs and it is for this 12 Step Program. Read it out loud before you begin your day or as you end your day. Use it as you will, and let the Spirit of the Most High God infuse you with his power.

ABOUT THE AUTHOR

Dr. Julia Floyd Jones earned a Ph.D. in Counseling Psychology from Texas Woman's University. She is a marketplace minister, prophetic painter, evangelist, teacher, and life coach. She is founder and president of Global Affairs Ministries and Artist and Scribe, LLC.

12 Steps To Overcoming Tragic Life Events, written by Dr. Jones is a manual that will help you get over your past and teaches the fundamentals of Christianity. It is the first part of *Seek Ye First The Kingdom Of God* and is available from the publisher and all online booksellers.

For more information or to contact the author please visit www.artistandscribe.com.

REFERENCES

Apostle Paul's Missionary Journey. htttp://www.ccel.org/bible/Phillips/cno92maps1.h (accessed October 1, 2013).

Munroe, Myles (2006). *Kingdom Principles Preparing For Kingdom Experience And Expansion (pp. 180-182).* Shippensburg, PA: Destiny Image Publishers, Inc.

Pierce, Chuck D. (2011). *A Time To Advance Understanding the Significance of the Hebrew Tribes and Months (pp. 257-320).* Denton, TX: Glory of Zion International, Inc.

Price, Paula A. (2006). *The Prophet's Dictionary The Ultimate Guide to Supernatural Wisdom.* New Kensington, PA: Whitaker House.

Strong, James (1990). *The New Strong's Exhaustive Concordance Of The Bible.* Nashville, TN: Thomas Nelson Publishers.

The Exodus. http//www.bible-history.com/maps/route_exodus (accessed July 12, 2013).

The Holy Bible, King James Version. Thomas Nelson, Inc.

The King James Study Bible (1988). Liberty University.

The Merriam-Webster Dictionary (1998). Merriam-Webster, Inc.

Trimm, Cindy (2008). *The Rules Of Engagement The Art of Strategic Prayer And Spiritual Warfare (pp. 53, 54, 83).* Lake Mary, FL: Charisma House.

Printed in the United States
By Bookmasters